INTO THE

WOODS

by

MINDFUL WRITERS
RETREAT AUTHORS

Into the Woods contains nonfiction and fiction pieces. In the fictionalized pieces, names, characters, places, and incidents are the product of the authors' imaginations or are used fictitiously. Any resemblance to actual events, locales, or persons, living or dead, is entirely coincidental.

ISBN-13 978-1986913331
ISBN-10 198691333

EIRA by Wende Dikec
THE BUTTERFLY WALL by Hilary Hauck
THE ELF DOOR by Eileen Enwright Hodgetts
A NEW MIND by Larry Ivkovich
A LIGHT IN THE WOODS by Lori M. Jones
IN THE DARKNESS OF THE WOODS by Kimberly Kurth Gray
LIGHT OF THE MOON by Ramona DeFelice Long
LINGERING MEMORY by MaryAlice Meli
WALKING THE PLANK by Gail Oare
THE LAST FAMILY VACATION by Kim Pierson
GENEVA: INTO THE WOODS by Cara Reinard
TRAIN WRECK by Kathleen Shoop
A MINDFUL CHANGE by Martha Swiss
A HIKE THROUGH THE WOODS by Madhu Bazaz Wangu
I NOURISH THE UNIVERSE AND THE UNIVERSE NOURISHES ME by Madhu Bazaz Wangu
THE GIRL IN ROOM 9 by Lorraine Bonzelet
FEAR OF FAILURE by Selah Gray
CONSECRATION by Laura Lovic-Lindsay
WHAT I DON'T KNOW ABOUT NATURE by Ramona DeFelice Long
WISP OF THE FOREST by Larry Schardt
FOREST BATHING by Martha Swiss
THE HOUR HAS COME by Amy Walter

SAVING THE SYCAMORES by Teresa Futrick
TO BOLDLY GO…INTO THE WOODS by Sherren
Elias Pensiero
OUT OF THE WOODS by James Robinson, Jr.
YOU'VE GOT MAIL! by Linda K. Schmitmeyer
INTO THE WOODS by Carol Schoenig
INTO THE WOODS: LESSONS LEARNED AND
LOVED by Denise Weaver
THE DIRTIEST, MOST DIVINE SANCTUARY, INTO
THE WOODS by Michele Zirkle
WALK IN THE WOODS by Gail Oare
WALKING MEDITATION by Lori Jones

Cover design: Eva Talia at www.evataliadesigns.com

Interior: Rachelle Ayala

INTRODUCTION
by Kathleen Shoop

"Live in the sunshine, swim in the sea, drink the wild air."
--Ralph Waldo Emerson

Into the Woods is the title and theme for this assortment of short stories, poems, essays, music, and one walking meditation. Each piece is unique in tone and genre and the result is that the collection captures the fascinating, frightening, fun, healing, and fantastical wonder of time spent in the woods. The twenty-six contributors who attend Mindful Writers Retreats in the highlands of Ligonier, Pennsylvania, are donating 100 percent of the proceeds to support the research and work of The Children's Heart Foundation.

Mindfulness and Writing

Before there were Mindful Writers Retreats in the Laurel Highlands woods, there was Madhu Bazaz Wangu in solitary bliss developing meditations to help writers become more mindful and purposeful in meaningful ways. What is mindfulness? Madhu describes it as, "Being attentive. Meditation practice teaches mindfulness. Mindfulness is a combination of many qualities such as awareness, being still, listening to silence, slowing down, focusing on one task at a time, being attuned to our senses, and being sensitive and kind to others." Through decades of meditation, Madhu found that it enriched her writing.

"Like meditation, writing requires dedication and devotion. The reason it takes time to warm up before writing is because we have so much mental clutter. When we meditate, petty thoughts and sentimentality settle down. Meditation trains the practitioner to accept things as they are. It strengthens intention, determination and finally persuades the writer to act. When writers focus on breathing they learn to concentrate and remove mental obstructions that let imagination flow and their unique voices to surface." Who doesn't want to find and strengthen their unique voice?

In 2009, Madhu held her first workshops to teach writers meditation so they could experience what she'd been learning for years. Soon she invited people to meditate as a group and then stay and write together. The result was that authors not only improved the quality and volume of writing but writing with others infused the process with inspiration and a sense of community that is often lacking when writing is your job.

Madhu filled a need that most writers hadn't considered important before they were invited into the group. She found that "Writing with other writers transports each to a higher level of consciousness. This is not like people mechanically packing meat in a factory or cutting car doors at Ford Motor Company plant. It is participating in an unseen aura that enriches all the participants. There is an overpowering energy that comes from communities, the same passion that ardent pilgrims feel on their sacred journey together." A community was born!

Mindful Writers Retreats

Madhu's writing groups grew in number as writers discovered the degree to which mindfulness enhanced their writing. I was a weekly attendee and found the day groups changed my writing process significantly. In addition to sitting meditation enriching my writing, Lori Jones and I discussed the way that we both experienced mindfulness that influenced our writing when walking, running or swimming for exercise. I proposed the idea of a writing retreat that combined Madhu's sitting meditations and mindful walking in the woods. Madhu was hesitant about the idea, wondering if days full of nothing but writing, meditating and walking were too much for people to commit to.

"Why would they come?" Madhu asked.
"Why *wouldn't* they?" I asked.

And so Madhu and I began to plan. We put Madhu's *Meditations for Mindful Writers Volumes I and II* (led by Madhu when she is present), walking meditation (led by Lori Jones), shared meals, and days of writing at the heart of the retreat and we crossed our fingers that writers would come. They did!

Nine retreats later, scores of writers from seven states have attended. Over the same period Mindful Writers Retreat Authors have published a plethora of works including essays, articles, poems, stories, books, and more. Now I coordinate the retreats with Larry Schardt. Over time we've considered adding and removing various elements of the retreat, but we always remain true to the core purpose and activities that were initially put in place. We've added a third retreat per year and have a waiting list at times. The retreats are held in the Laurel Highlands of Western Pennsylvania at the Ligonier Camp and Conference Center, creating a unique opportunity for committed writers. At the retreats, authors leave writing business, household obligations, and personal lives behind.

Somehow, even with the five days being filled with massive amounts of writing all day and into each night, we leave the retreat energized. Projects are started, fleshed out or completed. Extended writing, meditation and walking gives new ideas the space to emerge. Problems are solved, friendships made, networks strengthened and the surety that we must go back again takes hold. There's nothing like the retreats for shedding regular life and welcoming a gentle yet laser-sharp focus on work that's neglected far too often.

Why an anthology? Why call it *Into the Woods*?

We write together a lot—in person and online. All of the contributors attend Mindful Writers Retreats. Some write together once a week in clusters around Pennsylvania or in the Online Mindful Writers Group on Facebook. After years of retreating together we decided it was time to create something, a sound bite of the variety of voices that make up the group.

An anthology is a fabulous way for authors to pool their energy into a project while maintaining independence in what each person produces for the book. It's fun! The collection creates a unique and vibrant body of work that can be read in short spurts or in its entirety. The theme—*Into the Woods*—seemed like the perfect idea for the Mindful Writers Retreat Authors' first collaboration since so much inspiration, so many ideas, so much wonder has grown out of our quiet times in the lovely woods.

Why Raise Money for The Children's Heart Foundation?

One hundred percent of proceeds will go to support the research and work of The Children's Heart Foundation (CHF). It's the country's leading organization solely dedicated to funding research for congenital heart defects. CHD is the number one birth defect in the world, impacting approximately 1 in 100 births or 40,000 babies a year in the U.S. There are about forty known defects with no known cure for any of them. CHD is the leading cause of infant death due to birth defects.

Since it was founded in 1996, The CHF has funded over 10.6 million dollars in independent research projects, as well as funding projects in collaboration with the American Heart Association. One of our anthology authors (and original Mindful Writers), Lori Jones, runs the Pennsylvania Chapter because her own daughter, Riley, was born with a CHD twelve years ago. The CHF funded a stem cell research project a few years ago that provided the seed money to begin working toward a cure for her daughter's defect, Complete Heart Block. Thanks to the advances in research, there has been a 30 percent decline in death rates from CHD over the last decade.

Our love and concern for Lori and her family are a natural outgrowth of spending so much time with her. But the work she does on behalf of other children and their families has inspired us all to learn more about the work of the CHF. There's so much need, and so many solutions if only there was enough money to fund the research. Thank you to all the readers whose purchase of this book will help ensure that research and treatment options get Riley closer to a cure, that all those impacted by CHD can live long, healthy, vibrant lives.

"Yes, there are bold ones who fearlessly venture into the sky with triple toe loops or spin off mountain tops on thin boards, and even men unflinching enough to pick up brooms and sweep their way to gold, but there's no group more daring than writers who are open to annyyythinnnnggg…" - Gail Oare, Mindful Writer

Acknowledgements

We owe so much gratitude to Larry Ivkovich! Your input and collaboration were priceless (therefore no monetary amount can be attached or collected). Your help with cover design decisions streamlined the process. And, your work in shepherding, organizing and analyzing the writings as they were submitted lightened the load and made the development of *Into the Woods* so much fun.

An enormous thank you to Madhu Bazaz Wangu for all that you've done to create the content that anchors the other elements of the retreat. Your lifelong dedication to meditation, education, writing and scholarship has transformed countless authors' writing lives. Your generosity in sharing it all is inspiring.

Thanks so very much to "Rock 'n' Roll" Larry Schardt! You've helped to ensure that the retreats are bi-annual and now tri-annual events. Your work in managing the logistics of the retreat has made it possible for me to more easily work on the theme and materials for each event.

The amount of time it takes to wrangle the details related to registration, dietary restrictions, menus, and more into submission is always surprising! Thank you, Larry for the work, friendship and laughter!

How to thank Lori Jones? Your walking meditations, dedication to Mindful Writers, and lovely gifts to lure the writers out of bed before dawn breaks have made all the difference! Thank you for teaching new retreaters how walking meditation can change their writing process as well as the writing itself. As an extra special thank you, we will do our best to raise tons o' cash for CHF! You, Riley, and your entire family live deep in all our hearts.

Many million thank yous to Wende Dikec! You listen to every word about the retreat plans and then pretend to be surprised when you arrive—can't put a price on that. Your support at every turn, loyal friendship, and infectious humor make planning the retreat and going to it more fun and productive than I ever imagined possible. Alexander House Rules!

Thanks to every writer who attends the retreats! Each week spent writing is so much more productive because of all of you. Just looking around at the retreat, the variety of writers and people is obvious: the neat-nicks with tables boasting only a laptop, a notebook, and a tidy row of pens, the messy tables splattered with crumbs, towers of research, and a smattering of note cards, the walkers, the runners, plodders and gazelles, those lying in the grass, the quiet as mice writers, laugh-out-louders... It all only begins to hint at the diversity of writing represented in the group. Awardees, bestsellers, self-published, traditionally published, hybrid, not-yet-released, not-yet-signed, bloggers, sci-fi, fantasy, historical, non-fiction, poetry, romance of every sort, literary, memoir, and more. At Mindful Writers Retreats the labels don't create a hierarchy, but they do reveal the richness of those who attend. Every single writer is like family. Every single writer contributes to the magic and the fun of the week simply by committing to the writing. We can't wait for the next retreat and the next and the next. Happy writing until we meet again. Thanks also to all those who contributed to the anthology. It's fantastic to know we'll make a difference in a fellow writer's life.

Truckloads of thank yous must go to the staff at the Ligonier Camp and Conference Center. Each and every person is kind and giving and never fails to smile and lend a hand when planning and when the retreat is underway. Your little spot in the Laurel Highlands is heaven and what a gift it is that you share it all with us.

Thank you to Kim Pierson, Lori Jones, and Larry Ivkovich for your awesome reads at the end of the publication road.

Thank you so very much to Eva Talia. Your cover designs are gorgeous and you are so easy to work with. Thank you for making sure what wraps this collection is as wonderful as what's in it.

Rachelle Ayala—thank you for your wonderful formatting and quick turnaround. We appreciate you being there for us!

Marlene Engel and Julie Burns—thanks to both of you for your fabulous proofreading and for your faster than light turnaround. Having each of you read and find all those pesky typos and text issues is so reassuring.

And last but definitely not least...

We couldn't have published the anthology without the generous and skillful editing work of Ramona DeFelice Long. The gift of your expertise, wisdom, and enthusiasm has made the collection stronger than it ever would have been without you. We're so grateful that you're our treasured friend, part of Mindful Writers, and that you could fit *Into the Woods* into your tight as a drum editing schedule.

Table of Contents

SHORT STORIES

EIRA
by Wende Dikec

The lights went out, and Eira held her breath, waiting for the emergency generator to work. It started with a shudder and a horrific crunching noise, but at least it continued to function.

She closed her eyes, feeling the fear in her chest ease when she heard the comforting sound of the humming engine. She couldn't bear the thought of being left cold and alone in the dark.

Tugging her pale, blond hair into a ponytail, she pulled her ragged wool cardigan tightly across her body and walked over to the window of Alexander House, a grand name for such a Spartan hunting cabin, to peek outside. She waited for the sun to come up, looking out the dirty glass pane, and continued to stare out the window long after the sun rose in the sky. She didn't know why she bothered. She saw nothing outside except the same white expanse she'd seen every day for the last five lonely months.

Eira opened the door to grab some wood from the pile for her fire, her body flinching from the chill of the icy wind. She had enough wood to last a few more weeks, and then she'd have to make the dangerous trip into the forest to chop more. She dreaded it, but not as much as she dreaded living without the generator. If she rationed carefully, she'd have enough fuel for another month, but she wasn't sure what she'd do after that. She hadn't planned on being stranded for such a long time. Spring should have arrived almost two months ago.

She blinked in surprise when she saw a figure moving toward her house, struggling in the waist deep snow. Eira squinted against the harsh sunlight reflecting off the white landscape, trying to make out if the approaching form was human or animal, friend or foe, but she could see very little at this distance. She stumbled back into her warm little house, and reached for her heavy coat. She quickly slipped on her snowshoes before grabbing her gun, a nervous sense of excitement building inside her. If it was a person, it would be the first human being she'd seen in months. If it was an animal, she'd shoot it and have food for a week. And if it was one of the strange ones, the creatures that were no longer human yet not completely animal, she'd kill it without remorse and leave its carcass for the hungry bears to find.

She waited on her front porch, her gun ready as it came closer. It looked human, bundled under layers of heavy clothing, but she wasn't taking any chances.

"Who are you?" she asked, her voice echoing in the quiet wilderness.

The figure stopped moving and looked directly at her. She could see a dark beard covering the skin exposed beneath protective ski goggles. It was a man.

"My name is Ben," he said, his voice sounding scratchy and strange, as if it hadn't been used in a long time. "I saw the smoke from your fire. Can I come in and warm up?"

Eira paused, considering his request. He seemed human enough, but it was a risk. He could steal her food, hurt her, or take her precious fuel. She weighed her options quickly. Loneliness won out over caution, but she wasn't stupid. She clenched her gun as she waved him in.

Ben was so tall he had to bend over to enter the cabin. Eira walked in behind him, shutting the door. He looked around as he removed layer after layer of clothing, starting with the heavy, tinted ski goggles. When he got down to a thick wool sweater and jeans, he turned to face her.

"You alone up here?" he asked incredulously.

Eira didn't say anything. She tightened her grip on the gun and stared coldly into his brown eyes. He shook his head, as if admonishing himself. "Sorry. You don't have to answer. I was simply surprised. I haven't seen another person in months, not even in Pittsburgh."

Eira blinked. "No people in Pittsburgh?" After finding the nearby town of Ligonier completely deserted on the one trek she dared to make into the wilderness, Pittsburgh had been her only hope. Now, it seemed, even that was no longer a possibility.

Ben held out his reddened hands to the fire, a sad, resigned expression on his face. "Pittsburgh was a ghost town," he said. "Unless you count the crazy ones." He let out a dry chuckle that sounded more like a sob. "I always thought having cabin fever meant you were bored. I never knew it could be an actual sickness, that being trapped in the ice and snow could make a person lose their mind." He gave her a long, assessing look, his eyes lingering on the gun still held in her hands. "What's your name?" he asked softly.

"Eira."

He chuckled. "Appropriate. A Norse goddess, right? It fits with all this snow."

She shifted her weight, uncomfortable, as she tried to keep the gun steady. "I guess," she said. "It could have been worse. They almost named me Elsa."

He laughed, tossing back his head. The sound penetrated the wall she'd erected around herself. It had been so long since she'd heard anyone laugh. It brought on a wave of emotion that was both agonizing and sweet, and she fought against the force of it as she blinked away tears.

"I'm not going to hurt you, Eira," he said, his voice gentle.

Decision made, she slowly lowered the gun, putting the safety on before she set it aside, still within reach. He watched her, letting out a long breath.

"How long have you been here?" he asked, sitting down on one of the comfy chairs next to the hearth.

Eira took off her coat and brushed the hair out of her eyes. She usually kept it neatly plaited, but it had grown, the silky strands nearly reaching the middle of her back.

"Since before Christmas," she said. "I was on winter break from college, and my parents and brother were going to meet me here. They…they didn't make it to the cabin on time. I arrived just before it started. They left a few hours too late, but I'm sure they're okay. They have to be okay."

Ben nodded in understanding. "The storm of the century," he murmured. "Well, that's what they called it, until they figured out it was no storm at all, and we'd just entered into another ice age."

Eira sat on her rocking chair, only a few feet away from Ben, and leaned forward, hands on her knees. "Can you tell me what's going on?" she asked, hearing the desperation in her own voice. "I need to know, even if it's bad. I don't have a television here, and I haven't picked up anything on my radio in ages."

Ben ran a hand through his hair, and Eira was surprised to realize he wasn't much older than she. She hadn't noticed it because of his shaggy beard and the haggard and weary expression he wore. As she waited for him to speak, she poured some hot water into a cup and made him some of her precious tea. The coffee had run out long ago. He reached for the cup gratefully, and took a long sip.

"There is no television anymore," he said. "No radio. It's a mess out there. Roads are impassable. People are starving. The government is in ruins. Half the people are crazy, plagued with cabin fever. Scientists say it's an actual illness, a bacterial infection of the brain, but I don't know. Have you seen any people like that around here?"

"Once," she said. "A man came here. He acted like an animal. He couldn't speak. He was filthy and sick. He died right outside my door." She didn't bother explaining that a bullet from her gun had been what killed him.

Ben glanced at her, admiration glowing in his dark eyes. "How on earth did you manage to make it on your own this long?"

"My dad taught survival training to soldiers," she said. "He made sure my brother and I could take care of ourselves."

Ben nodded, taking another sip of the hot tea. "He taught you well. I grew up in Alaska, so this is nothing new for me," he said with a smile. "Snow, snow, and more snow. I moved south, thinking I was getting away from it. No such luck."

"What will you do now?" asked Eira, almost afraid to hear the answer.

He sighed. "I don't know. I think the best option is to keep heading south. I've heard there are some settlements along the Mexican border. Do you want to come with me?" he asked.

The air in the cabin felt still as he waited for her response. "I'm safe here," she said.

"For how long?" he asked. "You're going to need more supplies eventually. How are you going to get them on your own?"

Eira's stomach formed a tight knot at the thought of leaving. "But my parents and my brother might come any day now. You made it here. They could make it here, too."

He jabbed at the fire with the metal poker she kept next to the stone hearth. "I found you by pure blind luck. I thought Camp Ligonier was a military base," he said, giving her a wry smile. "I had no idea it was a conference center. The only good that came of it was seeing the smoke from your cabin, but it took me a few days to make my way up here."

She frowned. "Why did it take you so long? The lodge isn't that far away."

She'd cleaned out the supplies in the lodge ages ago, and carried them up to her cabin using an old door as a sled. She would have stayed in the lodge, but it was larger and much harder to heat and to defend. The cabin had one door, which meant one way in and one way out. The lodge, with its large windows looking over the valley below and its many doors, didn't feel as safe or as cozy as Alexander House. And, although she loved the stone fireplace in the lodge and the gleaming slate floors, she'd never be able to gather enough wood to heat it.

"Well, I had some visitors," he said.

"Who?"

"Bears," he said, with a wry smile. "Those poor confused, starving creatures. They stood right outside the door, growling at me. Refusing to leave. I had a long conversation with them, trying to convince them I wasn't very tasty. Finally, hunger drove them to seek out an easier meal."

She nodded. "They came out of hibernation to this," she said, waving a hand toward the window.

"When the bears finally decided to leave, it was night and I didn't want to risk it. I waited until this morning, so I could see where I was walking."

Eira understood his caution. In this new world, a broken bone could be a death sentence. "Then you found me."

"Then I found you," he said, with a smile that disarmed her, throwing her off kilter.

Could she trust him? *Should* she trust him? Her very life depended on her making the right decision, but her inner compass, the thing she'd depended on all her life, seemed to be malfunctioning. Desperation and loneliness made her weak, and she had to factor that into her choices.

"This place is isolated, Eira. I understand it makes you feel safe to stay here, but for how long?"

"The first rule of survival is to find shelter and stay in one place until someone can rescue you," she said, repeating the words her father had instilled in her long, long ago.

"What if no one's *left* to rescue you?"

He reached out to touch her arm, and Eira jumped, backing away. "Survival is key," she said, her mouth set in a narrow line. "Survival is my only option."

She remembered the last time she'd spoken with her father. He'd called her from his cell phone when he realized how bad the snow was getting, and he'd made her promise she'd hunker down and ride out the storm.

"You know what to do," he'd said. "We'll be there soon. I promise. Just keep your head straight."

But he hadn't come, and she was so tired of doing this alone, of being afraid, of not seeing another human face. Her head wasn't straight if she was even considering Ben's proposal, but the idea of being alone any longer terrified her more than the idea of the beasts and monsters outside her door.

"Surviving isn't living," he said, sadly. She stared at him, unable to respond. He took another sip of his tea. "But you don't have to decide right now. There is no rush. I can hunker down in the lodge until you make your choice. I kind of took a fancy to that Pittsburgh Steelers room. I was quite comfortable there…when the bears weren't trying to eat me, of course."

He gave her a wink and a smile. She ducked her head. "Or you could stay here. With me. I have enough room."

The light from the fire cast odd shadows over his face. "You sure?"

She gave him a single, curt nod. "I am."

He moved into her brother's room, and within days they'd established a fairly comfortable routine. Eira woke each morning with a new lightness in her heart, knowing Ben would greet her with a cheery wave, and make her a cup of tea. He teased her about her name, blaming her for all the snow.

"Can you please turn it off, goddess? We've had enough already."

At first she responded to his jokes with the ghost of a smile. A sense of numbness, of distance, overwhelmed her. It felt like she'd been buried in a kind of permafrost, much like the world outside her doorstep. Even moving the muscles of her face to form something as simple as a smile seemed impossible at first, like ice flowed through her veins instead of blood, but slowly, steadily that began to change.

One day Ben managed to kill a rabbit for their dinner. Eira made stew and stirred it at the stove. As the aroma of the cooking meat wafted through Alexander House, he acted out how he'd caught the rabbit, doing a spot-on Elmer Fudd impersonation, and that's when it happened...Eira began to laugh, a bursting, joyous sound.

Seeing the shocked expression on Ben's face, she stopped, the laughter dying in her throat, as she covered her mouth with her hand. Had she forgotten, even for a moment, that her parents and brother might be dead? That the world was now covered in snow? That she had nothing to live for, and had no joy left in her pitiful life?

She had. For that brief instance, she'd forgotten everything and everyone, and somehow that felt very wrong.

She turned back to the stew, her shoulders slumped, her heart heavy once again. Snow began to fall outside, as tears slowly rolled down her face.

Ben came up behind her, putting his hands on her arms and turning her around. When she refused to look up at him, he put his finger under her chin, and tilted it until her gaze met his.

"Don't feel guilty you're alive, Eira. Don't feel sorry if you're happy. What else do we have in this stupid, stinking world if we don't have that?"

She nodded, her thoughts swirling like the snow as she tried to find a way to respond. "I'm trying. It's...hard."

Such a small word to encompass so many things. If only she'd waited and come with her parents instead of driving straight from school. If only they'd left sooner and made it before the snow. If only they'd stayed at home this Christmas and not taken their annual trek to Alexander House. If only. If only.

She sighed. No, they would never have skipped Christmas at Alexander House. It meant too much to all of them. Tramping through the forest, axe in hand, to bring back the perfect tree. Baking with her mother and taking long hikes through the wilderness with her dad. Playing board games with her brother as her father sang along to Christmas music, off key as always.

They would never have skipped Christmas in their little cabin. It was what they did, an Alexander family tradition. No amount of snow would take away the memories they'd shared here. And no amount of "if only" would change the decision she had to make. They were running out of fuel and food. What would have lasted a month for one person, would only last a few weeks for two. She knew what she had to do, but she just needed to find the courage to say the words.

I'll go with you.

She'd practiced them over and over again, but couldn't quite manage to get them out. Maybe tonight would be the night. After they ate their stew, and sat by the fire to read a book aloud and chat together, maybe she would tell him then.

"Dinner will be ready soon," she said, turning back to the stew. And that's when she saw it. His knife. The one he must have used to clean the rabbit. The one she'd never noticed before.

She leaned over and picked it up, her heart pounding. "Where did you get this?"

He frowned, his dark eyebrows drawing together. "My knife? I've had it for ages."

She stared at him, deep into his eyes, and that's when she saw it. He was lying. She clenched the knife in her hand, the feel of it as comfortable as a pair of well-worn shoes. Of course it was familiar. She'd carved the hilt herself.

Her father's knife. The one he always carried strapped to his belt. The one thing he'd never leave behind.

"The truth," she said, her words coming through clenched teeth. "Now."

He sank into the chair, and put his face in his hands. She waited, as the snow outside turned into a blizzard and the wolves from high atop the mountain began to howl.

"I found it," he said, finally. "I found…him."

"My dad?"

He nodded. "He was sick. Cabin fever. But he wasn't fully changed yet. He could still speak, was still somewhat human, but he didn't have long. I could tell just by looking at him."

"What did you do?"

"I found shelter, an old barn, and managed to make a fire inside without burning the whole thing down. I wrapped him in blankets and gave him some water. There was really nothing else I could do. I just stayed with him, and listened to him talk."

"What did he say?"

"Well, he rambled, mostly. But then he started talking about you. How he needed to get to you. He knew you'd survive. 'She's Eira,' he said over and over again. 'Winter can't kill a Norse goddess.' And then he told me how to find you. He said you had supplies. In the morning, when I woke up, he was gone. I'm sorry, Eira."

"He was gone?"

"There was nothing I could do." He swallowed hard. "In all honesty, I came here, hoping you hadn't made it. I wanted your supplies, your food, your cozy little cabin. But then I met you, and my plans changed."

She laughed, and this time there was no joy in the sound. "Your plans changed." She stood up and looked out the window. The snow now fell as thick as a curtain, blocking her view outside. "Did you use his own knife to kill him?"

"Kill him…?"

"He promised he'd come for me, and he never breaks his promises. Even sick, he would have made it here. Only death could keep him away."

Ben rubbed a hand over his eyes. "It was the humane thing to do, Eira."

She put the knife in her belt, stuck her feet in her boots, and grabbed her coat off the peg next to the door. "Where is the barn?"

He stared at her. "You can't be serious. Look outside."

"I don't expect you to come, but I need to bring him back. He deserves a proper funeral. You would have done him a favor if you'd burned the barn down. A pyre would have been fitting. Otherwise, how can he make it to the afterlife? I have to help him."

He sank into the chair in front of the fire. "It's two miles away, just on the edge of town, but you'll never make it. If the bears don't get you, the cold will."

She smiled at him, but her eyes were ice. "I am Eira. I am snow. And I'm bringing my father home."

IN THE DARKNESS OF THE WOODS
by Kimberly Kurth Gray

It was in the woods I learned to be both afraid and brave. I knew better than to wander from our home out into the dark night where the thickness of the trees kept even a glimmer of moonlight from seeping through. There were bears and snakes, of that I was certain—but it was the gray misty figures that manifested in the night—those were the creatures to beware. I'd sit in bed, my face pressed against the window, and watch as they'd materialize from whiffs of smoke that rose from the ground like fog. They would fold themselves up like bats if the night's silence was broken.

"It's a terrible dream, sweetheart," Mother would say and hold me close to comfort me when I cried out in the night.

"There's nothing to fear from the dead, it's the living who are worrisome," said Father when I'd asked him if there were ghosts in the woods.

As the weeks passed, the gray mist gained volume and grew closer to our house. I tried to warn my parents, yet they failed to believe me. Then Annalise Gilbert went missing. Her clothes were found at the edge of the woods, lying in a puddle as if she'd evaporated.

The fathers of our town formed a search party and roamed the woods from sunrise to sunset for a week. No further trace of Annalise was found. I sat night after night staring into the inky blackness trying to see if any of the forms that appeared before me took the shape of Annalise.

"What's a coven?" I asked my parents one evening as we sat around the great oak table eating our supper. They look dumbfounded. Each sat with their mouth agape and their spoon in midair as drips of stew plopped to the table. Moments passed before either of them spoke.

"A coven is a group of witches," Father finally managed to say. Mother nodded slightly in agreement.

"Margaret Hamilton says the coven in the woods has taken Annalise as one of their own," I said, repeating what my arch nemesis had announced in our school room that morning. It seemed to me that evil Margaret would make a better witch.

"What nonsense," said Mother, regaining some of her composure. "Your father and I have told you before, Dorothy, the woods are dangerous and no place for little girls to be playing. There are wild animals living in there. I'm afraid poor Annalise encountered one."

"Do animals undress you before they eat you?" I asked, alarmed more at the thought of being seen naked than being eaten.

"No, of course they don't. Where do you ever get these ideas, Dorothy?" asked Mother.

"Then why were Annalise's clothes on the ground?"

"That will be enough, Dorothy," Father said, glancing toward Mother. Their eyes were dark and serious and I knew from now on they both would be much more careful about what was said in front of me. Neither of them mentioned Annalise again.

Each night I kept watch from my window. The pointy shapes blew in the breeze taking cover among the branches and sometimes lingering near our fence as if waiting for me. Did Annalise wait, too?

Several weeks passed, the fathers no longer searched and Annalise's name was barely mentioned other than as a cautionary tale. Father went to work at the railroad and Mother tended her garden and we talked of only pleasant things during mealtime. This did not stop me from wondering what had become of Annalise. Could a person really disappear into thin air? I worried endlessly that no one would search for me if I went missing.

I could not forget about Annalise. She stayed on my mind constantly. There had to be a way to find her. At night, after Mother and Father were long asleep, I would ease the window open and wait. Each night I inched the window open farther, hoping to tempt whatever was outside to come in. The gray haziness never moved beyond our fence.

I needed to see what was in the darkness of the woods. Father snored lightly as I tiptoed past the bed. Mother slept with one arm slung over her face as if she were as distressed in her dreams as she was when I misbehaved. I slowly opened the door and wedged a rock in the doorframe to keep it from shutting. The light of the moon guided me to our barn where I took a lantern and lit it the way Father had shown me. The air was heavy and I could feel the perspiration forming under my arms and trickling down my back.

I watched from the edge of the woods, waiting for the familiar gray smoke to appear, yet saw nothing. It would be easy to turn and run back home to my bed, but then I would never know what lived here and if they did indeed have Annalise. The smell of burning hair filled my nose and what felt like feathers brushed over my skin. I held the lantern high, bringing a great circle of light around me. Whatever was near fluttered away to the safety of the trees.

"And what is it that you want, little girl?" A thin raspy voice came from out of the darkness. I did not turn in its direction, but stood as still as my shaking limbs would allow.

"I've come for Annalise," I called out. A chorus of laughter bounced from the trees and wrapped around my body like vines. Panicked, I swung the lantern to and fro as they cowered in the dark crevices, hissing and shuddering. It was then I realized the light was their enemy. I turned to the right then to the left, brightening every space. Long gnarled nails, wide brims of hats, brittle gray hair, all of these they did their best to fold and hide away, yet they had been exposed.

"Let her go," I said. "Let Annalise go or I will burn these woods down." I picked up a branch and held it close to the flame. The wood began to crackle in my trembling hand and I could feel a fire igniting within me, one that I was prepared to release. My fear turned to anger and erupted from my body in a ferocious howl as the wind rose and swirled around me, dirt covering my eyes and branches scratching my skin. I no longer knew whether it was the wind or me who made the bellowing cries. Then all was quiet except for the sniffling of a small girl. Annalise lay naked, covered in ashes.

We walked quickly from the woods in the glow of the lantern, her hand clasped tightly in mine. Who could explain what had happened that night? Who would believe us? I knew then, however, it would not be my last encounter with witches.

THE BUTTERFLY WALL
by Hilary Hauck

Winter was arriving tomorrow, which meant by evening, Leotie's wall would be a kaleidoscope of butterfly wings, each set rolled into slender tubes of spiced reds and oranges.

Ever since the chief of the Dogwood, which was the kind of little person Leotie was, had appointed her guardian of the Great Spangled Fritillary wings, winter for her had become a time of mending and renewal, color and beauty, even if Lore said it was the season of sadness and defeat.

Sun edged her way up the other side of the hill. Leotie took her reed flute from its basket, and went to stand by the opening to her pine tree hollow. At the exact moment the first ray touched the drowsy shroud of morning, she breathed in the morning's expectation and wonder, then blew it into the flute to sound the melody of u-yv-tlv, song of winter, to call the butterflies home.

The notes scampered across the grass and joined with the song Una played at the door to her tree, then together the melodies tumbled in all directions to meet the chorus of other flutes until the entire pine grove rang. At the end of the chorus, Leotie transitioned into her butterfly verse, the kamama. Across the way, Una played to call the crickets, others played verses for beetles and ants, and all the insects who needed to be home before Winter nipped at their tarsus.

Winter had been a long time coming this year. Because the leaves were still rich green, they had not played the a-ta-ya song to mark the rustling and scattering of leaves on the old oak by the pond. No Frost had visited, so there had been no need to play the u-ya-dv-ha song.

In a normal year, butterflies would have drifted in, even on days when no song was played, some simply relieved at the chance to burrow to rest, others overburdened by the wishes people whispered to them throughout bright days of hope. They carried the wishes in secret and with great care, and when it was time to march deep into the winter rest, they whispered them to the good earth, to plant and grow the answers for the people to find.

At the end of the verses to the winter song, Leotie and the other little people played the chorus one more time to make sure it reached as far as every butterfly, near and far.

Leotie returned the flute to its basket and, for the umpteenth time, she checked that she had every nuance of colored silks she might possibly need to embroider repairs to the wings. Her stash of porcupine quill-tip needles stood tall in her new milkweed pincushion, and she had a good supply of saw grass blades to cut the silk. She checked every burdock spike set into the curved inner bark wall, climbing the pine cone steps to the very top. Everything was ready.

Bolstering for the work ahead, she sipped nectar from an acorn cap. It was particularly sweet this year, an upside of Winter being late. Then she went back to the door to wait. She probably ought to enjoy the moment of calm, but she'd had far too many moments of calm already. She was anxious to get started.

Sun was nearing the top of the crest and the webs cast to capture the returning insects were starting to glow with orbs of dew the earth had hung out to dry.

Leotie stuck her head a little farther out the door, but instead of a butterfly or cricket, two people were approaching from the lodge. There was no time to reach for pollen puffs to protect her ears against the deafening boom of their voices. She covered her ears. People weren't apt to know their nature, except the part of their nature that made them talk too much. Only these people weren't talking.

A dart of movement caught Leotie's eye. A straggly old cricket was lurching, rather than marching in. His back leg caught on a twig, toppling him off-balance. He crashed left and ended up in a tangle between the two trees.

He shook himself off and came straight for Leotie instead of Una, who stood in her doorway, flute still in hand. Crickets could be forgetful creatures.

Any other type of little person might have sent him on his way, but the nature of the Dogwood is to do things for others out of the goodness of their hearts, so Leotie sent a silent plea for the people to pass in silence, uncovered her ears, and offered him a ladle of nectar.

The cricket sipped, sat, and sighed.

"Welcome," Leotie said sincerely, but she looked pointedly over her shoulder at Una's tree, in a gentle reminder as to where the cricket should go.

"Ah, but I have a tragic tale. One I have no choice but to tell."

Tragic tales on butterfly day were inconvenient, but must be heard. But they should be heard by Una, too. Leotie gestured with her hand for her to join them.

"It all began some weeks ago when the sun shone and the sky blazoned." Crickets have never quite got the hang of a hook to a story, so Una had ample time to dash—fingers in ears—the treacherous stretch to Leotie's tree.

"Come." Leotie ushered them inside.

The cricket had not paused his story, but he was only just getting to the point. "I have no choice but to recount that the butterflies have simply gone mad. Seeing as Winter didn't see fit to follow his nature and come along, they shall stay out and flitter for as long as they please."

"But Winter *is* coming!" Una said.

"Ah, but if he comes, they'll say he didn't uphold his part, and so why in nature should they? Worse still," Cricket trundled on with his story, "the other insects have got wind of it and are thinking about joining the butterfly rebellion."

26

"We must get word to them without delay. Winter has instructed Frost to get here tomorrow, and you know how bitter he gets about being late."

"They'll scant believe you. Rumor has it that you'll use fear tactics to bring them in."

"But the secrets! No dreams will be planted."

"I'd stick around to help, but I'm a good bit tired, such is my nature. I'd be grateful to be put to rest."

"You need to cross to the next tree," Leotie said.

Una leaned out the doorway. "More people, a trail of them. We have no choice, we'll tend him here."

Leotie didn't hesitate. She handed Una a cloth dipped in witch hazel. One on either side, they rubbed Cricket down, head to wing tip to claw. Then they each took a stiff, leather forewing and unhooked them, being careful not to pull them apart at the tip. The hind wings had frayed edges and wrinkles, and on Leotie's side there was a singed hole.

"Got a bit too close to a firefly," Cricket explained.

Cricket trundled off through the wintering hole to take his rest, and Una carefully folded the hind wings into a fan, slung the forewings over her shoulder, and climbed to the top spike to hang them.

Leotie's wall of art would have one corner that was odd. A dot in the corner to start the matching color like punctuation, only at the start of a sentence. She didn't have the silk color of cricket wings, but there was no time to dwell, because Frost sent a howl of wind in warning of his bitterness, and they heard the tumble of another cricket. He shook himself off, but still came to Leotie's door with a half leaf on his back, his foot dragging a web.

"Welcome," Leotie said, looking pointedly at Una's tree past the cricket.

"Ah, but I have a tragic tale. One I have no choice but to tell."

"We have heard the tragic tale," Leotie said, firmly.

They ushered the cricket inside and to one side, because another cricket was stumbling over. That cricket, too, came to Leotie's, its tragic tale at the ready. Before long, they had five crickets at varying points of the tale, earnestly delivering their news.

"What do we do?" Una asked.

"We'll have to rest them here. We have no choice," Leotie said, and stopped herself from looking at her wall. There was still ample room for the butterflies, they would just have to make do. "We'll need more supplies."

"We will go." One of the crickets who had finished his story now reared on its back legs to emphasize his pride in his offer of help, and nearly fell into the crickets gathered behind him, the *we* Leotie supposed he was talking about.

As each cricket completed his story, Una thanked him profusely and sent him after the others with a list of what to bring from her tree. Even so, two of the crickets came back to ask what they were to collect again. Spikes from her wall, the tub of witch hazel and the other of nectar, all the silk thread and porcupine needles, she reminded them.

The crickets returned, and two began the task of nailing new spikes on open expanses of the wall.

The spring of an energetic cricket, then an onslaught of panicked arrivals began. All crickets. Leotie had little time to contemplate the new arrangement, because the crickets were tired and in need of tending.

In what seemed like no time at all, Sun knelt on the crest of the hilltop ready to slide down the other side. Day had passed, Moon did not plan to look in on them until early morning, and then just a sliver of a peek. A small cluster of crickets were left, no butterflies.

Light shone from moonflowers around the walls of the tree house. Leotie and Una gathered some from the far side and set them on the floor in front of the wall to see their work.

Rows of carefully hung cricket wings. Fan-folded hind wings first, then leather forewings over them. Rather like two leather petals, and a protruding stamen.

"They didn't come back," Leotie said, though Una could surely see that for herself.

"Ah, that's a tragic story," one of the crickets began. Leotie was sure this one had already told his tale, but she ushered him to the side of the door so he could tell it again in any case.

"But now is not the time for the same story, over again," Una warned over Leotie's shoulder.

"I'll announce it as a premise, then," the cricket seemed unusually compliant to shorten his story, "because I'd forgotten until you happened to mention it, the rest of them are in the top field. They've likely taken cover for the night, the fishers are out, they'll surely decimate any stragglers."

"But that's a new story!" Una said.

"And by dawn, Frost will be here and they'll not be able to fly!" Leotie said. And no secret dreams will be planted, and there'll be no wings for next year, she thought, but didn't dare say it out loud.

"We need some of you to stay up and help us with a rescue at dawn."

The same handful of young crickets that had helped with supplies conferred in cricket whispers, which were actually as loud as cricket normal voices, but nobody wanted to hurt their feelings by telling them that.

"We'll do it," one eventually announced, though Leotie and Una had already overheard their decision.

Leotie and Una and the crickets then took extra nectar, and sat around to spend the night waiting and telling tales. When it was time to start getting ready, Leotie felt a pang of Lore's Winter sadness. She knew she would miss them, because it never seemed to be the same crickets or butterflies who came back to be fitted for wings in spring or summer.

As the first rays meandered toward the valley, the crew of crickets and Dogwoods, their ears stuffed with pollen buds in case any humans were around, crept out of the hollow and across to the next tree. Mist had settled in the valley, laying in horizontal wisps, too sluggish in the morning chill to get up and reach for the clouds. Crystals decorated every leaf, twig, and stone, clamoring for attention and adoration, fidgeting with the excitement that any moment now, Sun would pull itself up on the hill and ignite their dazzling shine.

The band of rescuers spread out around the tree to look in all directions. Two people appeared at the edge of the pine grove, their footsteps crunching the iced walkway, but incredibly, they, too, passed without talking. Leotie led the procession to the next tree, trying to ignore Frost who groped at her legs. Again they spread out around the tree to check for danger from all sides—Cat had seen them. Leotie took some nectar balls out of her leaf bag as an offering. He sniffed them indignantly, then decided they would suffice. At the last tree at the grove's edge, they all breathed in an extra dose of morning wonder, and set out along the edge of the dirt road.

Air stung Leotie's cheeks, her fingers pinched in the cold, her feet stumbled on the rough terrain. But she did not pause. Una and the crickets must be struggling, too. If she faltered, they would falter.

They found the first butterfly at the bottom of the meadow, wings tight shut, legs flickering in the air. Leotie and Una breathed on his wings to thaw. It was no good, Frost had sewn them shut. A cricket loaded her on his back. They loaded three more frozen butterflies before they found the hollow.

Big Butterfly sat on a stone above the others. Leotie pulled the pollen puffs from her ears to listen.

"Ignore this mild Frost," he was saying. "Winter has skirted his duty, and therefore we should not be expected to do ours."

The scattering of butterflies murmured agreement, flickering their wings at a faster beat.

"It's worse than I thought," Leotie said. "I expected them to have seen reason by now."

She stepped into the hollow, Una and the crickets beside her.

"I have come to call you to rest, my friends. Perhaps you missed the song yesterday, it is time."

The butterflies turned toward her, some showing signs of weariness, defiant nonetheless. "Kind indeed, of you, but Winter has not come, and we, dear Dogwood, have decided not to rest," Big Butterfly said.

"I know you don't make decisions lightly, but I implore you. What of the wishes people have whispered to you all summer long? You need to carry them below to sow them if they are to grow next summer," Leotie pleaded.

"The people will have to make their *own* wishes come true."

"Our way, the Dogwood way, is if you do something for someone, do it out of the goodness of your heart. Can you not do the right thing even if someone else has not?"

"Butterflies are no more Dogwoods than crickets are butterflies."

"No, but you have your own true nature to abide by." Past the shelter of the hollow, Frost was howling with laughter.

"Why, if nobody else is abiding by theirs?"

"What if you're wrong? There are already butterflies out there with frozen wings. No wings, no butterflies, people will stop planting flowers, because they certainly won't do it for the slugs and bees."

"Some care about the bees," a slim butterfly who was shivering near the opening said, his voice timid.

"How do you know?" Big Butterfly asked.

"I know from their wishes."

More wind thrust air on its way, and the entire hollow shook with creaks and cracks as ice engulfed grass at its edges.

"The ones who walk, they wish for peace," Slim Butterfly continued. "They want it so much they are willing to go against their nature, that's why they are silent. Some have even started to hear the answers the woods whisper."

The butterflies began to edge away from Big Butterfly and around this new voice.

"And what does that prove? That the people are going against their nature, too!" Big Butterfly urged.

"Yes, but for the good of others," another retorted.

The group clustered more closely around Slim Butterfly. He backed away from the attention, and inadvertently stepped from the protection of the hollow. Frost didn't hesitate. It sewed his wings shut in an instant and he fell with a gentle tap on his side.

"Help him!" someone cried. Leotie tried to reach her but couldn't get through the chaos of butterflies rushing forward, but they, too, stepped out of the shelter and one by red-orange one, Frost felled them.

"Stop!" Leotie shouted, but concern was also a butterfly's nature, so more butterflies rushed to help, and more fell. "Do something!" she implored the butterfly on the stone. He simply looked flabbergasted at the scene of devastation, he did nothing. This was terrible.

This was the defeat Lore spoke about.

Leotie covered her eyes with her hands, unable to watch the butterflies succumb. When she looked up again, the crickets were moving. It took her a moment to understand what they were doing—lining up as a barricade to prevent any more butterflies from reaching the fallen. The panic stopped, a stunned kind of calm began to settle.

"Alas," Big Butterfly said. "We were mistaken. We must, after all, head to rest."

With good fortune, the remaining butterflies agreed.

The crickets were loaded with two injured butterflies each to Leotie's tree, then they returned for the others, who flitted their wings to ward off Frost.

Somehow, miraculously, they got them back to the tree without further misfortune.

Leotie and Una tended to the injured butterflies first, their wings too frozen to roll. They uttered profuse gratitude as they trundled off to winter rest.

They were already tending the luckier butterflies when, with a roar of anger, Winter battered into the tree. Panic ensued.

"Calm down!" Leotie shouted. "Let's hear what he has to say."

"You want to hear? Baaah!" Winter roared. "All the bad that's been strewn in my path, preventing me from coming. Air itself is conspiring against me. Not that it'll admit it. It claims it is the fault of the people, the molecules they pour into it. But does my wind not drive molecules away? My chill not freeze them in their tracks? Nobody will claim responsibility. But I'm here now, and I intend to catch up."

And with that, Winter flew out of the tree and up the hill. Silence hovered while everyone pondered what he had said.

Big Butterfly was next to set himself between Leotie and Una, and they began to rub him, antennae to wing to toe. "Thank you, indeed, for helping me make the right decision. To think, the wings we might've lost. I had no idea Winter, too, faced challenges."

"Perhaps next time, we should take care of our own natures before worrying about others," Leotie suggested.

"A fine idea, indeed!" And Big Butterfly strode off to rest.

As they tended the last of the crickets, Leotie and Una expressed *their* profuse gratitude. Once everyone was safely at rest, Leotie pulled over pine cone chairs and poured her and Una an acorn of nectar.

"It looks like I'll be staying here until spring," Una said.

Leotie looked at the pattern on the walls, top and bottom with cricket wings, because they were the first to arrive and the last to help, the middle bits interspersed with damaged and healthy butterfly wings, all hung hastily, unrolled and crooked.

"You know, I'd been so looking forward to the colors of my wall, I never thought it could look this spectacular."

"I thought there was nothing better than a full wall of cricket wings, but I love the change, too," Una agreed.

"So we'll both stay here, I'll mend the butterfly wings, you the cricket ones," Leotie said. "Unless we want to try each other's?"

"What if I sew it wrong, make a new wing pattern or something?"

"Then you'll create a new species. Sew them together you'll get a Great Speckled Crickillary."

They began to laugh, and when Dogwoods laughed, the forest paused to hear the beautiful sound—birds from their singing, deer from their grazing, squirrels from their foraging.

"This new color wall, is it going against our nature, do you think?" Una asked after a moment.

"I'd prefer to think of it as adapting in time of need," Leotie said, thoughtfully. "We should tree together next year, too."

"A splendid idea—indeed," Una agreed.

THE ELF DOOR
by Eileen Enwright Hodgetts

Moira heard the Highland pipes for the first time on the day they buried Jake. The sounds of her distant homeland were carried softly on the summer wind, riding on the clouds that gathered above the Ohio River.

Oh, the summer time is coming,
And the trees are sweetly blooming,
And the wild mountain thyme
Grows around the blooming heather.
Will you go, lassie, go?
And we'll all go together
To pull wild mountain thyme
All around the blooming heather,
Will you go, lassie, go?

She couldn't go, not on that day when the family was gathered downstairs. On that day her heart was in the Veterans Cemetery with the man who had enticed her from Scotland so many years before. She couldn't follow the pipes, but she could leave the house. The mourners—so many of them—needed hot dog buns, and toilet paper, and someone's baby needed diapers. *Would they ever leave? How many meals was she supposed to prepare?*

She slipped out of the back door and walked through the afternoon heat to the corner store. That was where and when she found the door. She glimpsed it lurking at the back of the shelf and felt a sudden, urgent impulse to take her glasses from her purse and examine the strange little object. It was curved and planked like a tiny church door and it had a shiny brass doorknob. The package contained nails to nail the door to the chosen tree. As she stared she was already imagining what that tree would look like. An oak, it would have to be an oak.

You're too big.
Of course I'm too big. This is a door for elves.
So you believe in elves?
No.
But you're wondering if you will ever be small enough?
Perhaps.
What makes you think you could be?
Every day since Jake died, I've grown smaller.
You are still too big.
Soon I'll be invisible. Just a pair of ghostly hands making food.
But not yet.

How this item had ended up in Mr. Ntagala's corner store was a mystery, or perhaps it was providence. Maybe a misplaced number on a SKU had brought it here to hide dispiritedly among the overpriced boxes of cereal, the windshield wiper fluid, and the individual packets of Kleenex. It should have been in a fancy gift shop where people with more money than sense came to buy gifts for people who already had everything they needed. Only a person who already had all necessary worldly possessions would require an elf door for their backyard tree. This door, made of copper and brass, had been manufactured to sell for a high price; the label declared it had a value of $55.00 and the label also revealed the number of times Mr. Ntagala had reduced the price. Now it was selling for $7.50.

Mr. Ntagala took her money and placed the door in a separate bag, keeping it away from the hot dog buns and the diapers.

She walked back past the ravine and heard the pipes again with their soft questioning.

Will ye go, lassie, go?

Not yet.

The ravine, precipitously steep and tangled, had never been logged to feed the steel mills or accommodate the housing boom. She imagined that the tall old trees, reaching up toward the daylight, had once been silent witnesses to the passing of moccasined feet. Somehow, they had endured the poisoned sulfurous air of the steel mills, and still they survived and spread their leaves to shelter what was left of the primordial undergrowth.

She touched the bag that contained the elf door.

Will ye go, lassie, go?

Not yet.

Summer came and went and grass grew over Jake's grave, but her house was still full of people. *I think they will never leave.*

The first snow came as promised by the weatherman and with it came the Highland pipes. The snow was the thick kind that obliterated footprints and draped the trees in beauty; the song was a tempting whisper carried on the wind that battered her window.

Will ye go, lassie, go?
And we'll all go together,
To pull wild mountain thyme
All among the blooming heather.

Moira stood at the window watching the falling snow until a crash from the ground floor brought her back to reality. She went reluctantly down the stairs to find out how many people had been sleeping in her house and what had made that expensive sounding noise.

A collapsed coffee table, spilled milk and demands for coffee and breakfast kept her busy for a long time but nothing could keep the sound of the pipes at bay. At last, with her hands over her ears to keep in the precious music, she fled the chaos of her kitchen and locked herself in the second floor bathroom.

Here, amid the jumble of wet towels and unwashed clothes, the words were crystal clear, undiminished by the thousand miles of cold Atlantic Ocean that stood between her and their source.

> *I will build my love a bower*
> *By yon cool crystal fountain*
> *And round it I will pile*
> *All the flowers o' the mountain*
> *Will ye go, lassie, go?*

She cleared mist from the window. The snow was still falling but the light was fading. She would have to leave now while no one was looking, while she still could, while the words were still with her.

An impatient voice whined at the bathroom door. "How long are you going to be?"

As long as I like, it's my house! She would never say it aloud; never remind them all that it was her house and not theirs. *Who were they?* Children, grandchildren, step grandchildren, someone's live-in lover (*And who said that live-in meant living in my house?*) a grandchild's boyfriend, babies, toddlers, crawling all over her house, opening the pantry, making free with her food, a fat boy sprawled in Jake's recliner. *Any minute now they will want to know what's for supper.* Nothing! There will be no supper because I won't be here, and none of you can even make a sandwich.

She slipped out of the bathroom and stepped over a crawling baby. She paused when she saw that the infant's erratic path was taking it toward the stairs. *Old habits of watchfulness die hard, but she would no longer be watching.* She picked up the child, boy or girl, she didn't know, and deposited it in a crib, and then she went to her own room, the smallest bedroom, and reached for the bag containing the door that she had purchased in the heat of a summer day.

She went down the back stairs, past the living room where her children and their accumulated hangers-on split their attention between the massive flickering TV screen and the blue glow of their phone screens. No one spoke, but two boys wrestled silently in front of the fireplace for control of an iPad. *Who were they?* She had no idea.

She found Jake's old coat hanging on a peg in the back hallway and wrapped herself in its plaid warmth. Even now, it carried Jake's scents. They were not pleasant scents: motor oil, cigarettes, and Halls cough drops, but they were the scents of a time now drifting into oblivion. Jake was gone and his grave was disappearing under a blanket of snow, just as she was disappearing, buried under the weight of her heedless offspring who had taken advantage of Jake's passing to fill the house to overflowing.

At the time of Jake's death, she had been too bereft to stop them and had even welcomed the noise and the life they brought to the house. Now it was too late. They had proved to their own satisfaction, if not to hers, that they were incapable of preparing their own food and providing a roof over their own heads. They had made themselves her responsibility and then they had made her invisible.

If no one knows you are there, are you truly there?

She pulled on her snow boots and trudged up the road to the ravine. The wind was rising, blowing in from the north, lake effect snow, the kind that would bury them for days.

The words battered at her as she walked in time to the skirling of the pipes.

I will range through the wilds
And the deep glen sae dreary
And return wi' their spoils
Tae the bower o' my dearie
Will ye go, lassie, go?

A gust of cold wind drew her mind away from the pipes. The wind carried another noise: the plaintive howling of a dog. She abandoned the heathery bower for a moment while she dwelled on the fury welling up inside her. They had put Jake's dog outside again! She turned her face back into the stinging wind and her anger was enough to keep her warm as she lurched forward.

Those little... She knew plenty of bad words although she was not one to say them aloud. She opened and closed her mouth, silently spewing venom into the cold wind and having it return to her mouth in the form of stinging snow pellets.

She was so very close to disappearing; nothing but that plaintive howling could have made her fight the words keeping time with the drumbeat of her heart.

Will ye go, lassie?
Not yet!

She knew she would find him outside the backdoor wondering why he had been banished; wondering where *she* was, *she* who always took care of him. He was a gray shaggy dog of indeterminate breed but she had asked Jake to name him Dougal.

"Why Dougal?" Jake asked.

"He reminds me of the old crofters at home."

"Scotland?"

"Aye."

"Do you still miss it?"

She saw the hurt in his eyes. All these years and he still didn't understand. Of course she missed the Highlands and the heather, and her own people, but she had chosen him, and his country.

"I don't miss it," she lied. "I just thought I'd like to hear one of the old names, and you wouldn't let me give the boys Scottish names."

He laughed; she laughed with him. No, she wouldn't name her sons Hamish, or Aidan, or even Dougal, but the shaggy gray dog could live with the name.

Dougal's plaintive howling made her wonder if he would survive without her. His shaggy coat would protect him from the cold, but what would protect him from neglect? Would he soon be as invisible as she was?

She opened the back door and Dougal slipped in beside her. Pamela was in the kitchen with a crying baby on her hip. With her hair scraped back in a lank ponytail, yellow at the ends but gray at the root, she looked every inch the grandmother she was, which made Moira a great-grandmother. Pamela held the baby out to her. Moira shook her head.

"Who put Dougal outside?"

"Tiffany says she's allergic."

Who was Tiffany: resident or visitor? What did it matter?

"If Tiffany's allergic she's the one who should be outside."

"Mom!"

Moira considered her daughter for a long thoughtful moment. "They'll make you disappear."

"Mom?"

"You'll be invisible."

As she pushed past Pamela, the baby reached out for her hair. The little fingers caught and snagged.

Yes, that's what they do. They snag you with little fingers, and their little lives, and their constant little needs. No more.

She pulled open a kitchen drawer and surveyed the contents, glad that she had returned. She would have gone without a hammer and then what would have happened? The door had nails and nails would require a hammer.

She turned with the hammer in her hand and saw her daughter flinch. Perhaps she looked as wild as she felt. Well, no matter; they had never seen her this way before, but this is how she would be remembered.

She heard her own voice singing.

"I will build my love a bower."

"Mom!"

"By yon cool crystal fountain."

"Mom, what are you doing? Put the hammer down."

"I'm going out."

"Where?"

"To pull wild mountain thyme."

"Have you been drinking?"

"No, I haven't. Have you?"

She saw the flush in her daughter's cheek and shook her head.

"It won't help, love."

"But Mom…"

"Dougal and I are going for a walk."

"In this weather?"

"I'm Scottish. We're tough."

She slammed the door behind her and hurried away so that Pamela would not be able to hear the sound of bagpipes carried on the wind that blew from the ravine. Dougal trotted beside her, ears and eyes alert, tail wagging. He could hear the pipes. Perhaps some distant ancestor had been a deerhound.

The road was deserted. She turned to look behind her. The snow was filling in her footsteps as fast as she made them. No one would know where she had gone. *Would they even look, or was she already invisible to them?* She came to the top of the ravine. The sun had almost set and the ravine was full of dark shadows but she knew where she was going. In the summer she had been too big but not now. Now she was the correct size. In fact, if she didn't hurry she would be too small. She felt for the hammer in her pocket. If she became much smaller, if the song became any louder, she would not even be able to hammer the door into place.

She plumped herself down in the snow and scooted down the steep hillside on her backside. No point in having a broken ankle now. How would she reach the mountain with a broken ankle? Dougal kept pace with her in a flurry of fur, flying snow and waving tail. His eyes were bright with delight. She hoped, oh she really hoped, that he would be small enough. *He had to be; she couldn't leave him behind.*

Here it was: the lone oak in a grove of maples. Its sturdy trunk made the maples seem nothing but spindly saplings, Johnny-come-latelies with no more than fifty years in their roots, while this oak could surely count in hundreds.

She took the hammer from her pocket and placed it carefully at the foot of the tree. She took off her gloves and fumbled with the plastic wrapping on the elf door. The nails were hard to grasp. What if she dropped one? She would never find it again in the snow and the almost complete dark. How many nails did she really need?

The hammer had grown heavy in her hand. *Of course.* She was shrinking. If she didn't hurry, she would be too small and weak to hammer in the nails. She felt Dougal's weight pressing against her as he investigated the plastic packet and the elf door. *Why was he so heavy?* Surely he was shrinking. *He must be.* To the fat boys and Tiffanies of this world he was as invisible as she was. He should be shrinking.

She knelt in the snow and pressed the plastic door against the tree trunk. It fit perfectly and it barely needed the nails to keep it in place. *Good thing, too.* The hammer was now really heavy but Dougal wasn't shrinking. *You have to come with me.*

With the fourth nail in place, she turned the brass doorknob and the door opened onto a little room where a peat fire burned in a wide hearth and a bed stood ready beneath a bright patchwork quilt. *Not the patchwork of the Appalachian women, just the plain, square patchwork of a Highland woman.*

The window beside the bed stood open and beyond the window was the distant shape of Ben Nevis, its slopes carpeted with purple heather. The pipers were coming closer.

Will ye go, lassie, go?

"Are you coming in?"

A man in a green cap stood in the doorway. *An elf, of course.* She knew she could cross the threshold. Tonight she would warm herself by the peat fire and sleep beneath the patchwork quilt and tomorrow she would go to the mountain.

Dougal! He was enormous. His legs were like furry tree trunks. His breath on her neck had the force and heat of one of the old blast furnaces along the Ohio. She remembered Jake showing her his hometown when she first arrived. *He had been so proud of the fire that lit the night, and the flames reflected in the dark river water.* The furnaces were still and quiet, as still and quiet as Jake in the Veterans Cemetery. *What was his legacy? Careless children who destroyed his house, a fat boy in his recliner, his dog left out in the cold, and his wife whose heart had returned to the Highlands.*

Dougal whimpered but he showed no sign of shrinking. *I have to go.*

She thought of Dougal limping home through the snow. Would anyone even let him in? Would Tiffany's allergies condemn him to a frozen death? Would a dead dog and a house of chaos be Jake's legacy?

No one knows I'm here. I left no footprints. I could freeze to death.

The little man seemed shocked when she closed the elf door in his face. He had prepared a room for her, lit the fire, made the bed, and even brought the pipers in from beyond the mountain. They had spent months calling to her and she had almost answered their call. She had almost given in to their magic, but Dougal had known better. He had known she wouldn't shrink. He had known that she would not permit the chaos to continue.

"Mom!"

A voice from the top of the ravine. Pamela! *She followed me!*

"I'm down here."

"I'm coming down."

"No, don't. You'll probably break your ankle. I'll come up."

"How?"

Moira stood upright with her hand on her hips. "I'm stronger than I look."

"I know."

Moira called out questions as she clambered up the icy slope. "Who is Tiffany?"

"Someone's girlfriend."

"We're getting rid of her."

"Okay."

"Who is the fat boy in the recliner?"

"One of your grandchildren."

"The recliner is mine. If he gets in it again, he's gone."

"Okay."

"Don't just say it; mean it."

"I do mean it."

Pamela reached out to pull her up the last few feet. "Welcome back, Mom."

A NEW MIND
by Larry Ivkovich

League of the Haudenosaunee or the Iroquois
Confederacy
An Introduction

With their Great Law of Peace, an inspiration for the United States Constitution, the League of the Haudenosaunee forged an alliance among Five Nations of Iroquois tribes--Mohawk, Onondaga, Oneida, Cayuga, and Seneca. The Tuscarora later joined as the Sixth Nation in what was collectively called the New Mind. Certain oral traditions describe the formation of the Five Tribes during a total solar eclipse in the twelfth century. This has often been categorized as the stuff of legend. But all legend is rooted in fact. And sometimes, that fact is completely unexpected.

Passage from *Native American Myth to Future History*
By Ayenwatha Bigtree
C.E. 2019

***

A shaman-warrior with snakes for hair, his body misshapen, his magic dark and powerful...

Beyond a doorway of brilliant red light, Hiawatha discerned a threat by an ancient evil.

A portal opening into another demesne, one of despair and death, a gateway to a realm of madness...

His feet firmly planted on sacred ground, Hiawatha knew he would make his stand here, in this time and place, against that evil.

But, fortunately, he wouldn't have to do it alone.

***

Cameron Greene grunted and jerked awake. He gasped, hungry for air, as if he'd been holding his breath. Confused, he blinked in sunlight too bright for early morning. His mind whirled with fantastic dream-images.

What the hell?

He raised his throbbing head from the ground though he didn't remember lying down. Yet, here he lay. Wherever "here" was. He'd been traversing one of the many woodland trails as part of the early morning Walking Meditation and...what? Had he fallen asleep? Blacked out?

A tingle rushed up the back of his neck; a momentary dizziness shot through him. He rubbed his eyes and propped himself up on his elbows. A warm breeze danced over him, bringing with it the sweet scent of mountain laurels.

He rose to a sitting position, ran a hand through his long, brown hair, and glanced to his left. He sat on a grassy bluff with a rocky ledge extending only a few feet away.

A beautiful, wide valley sprawled below the ledge. Lush, green forest covered the abutting hills. Where were the rainbow colors of mid-fall he'd been enjoying? The weather felt more summer-like than autumnal. It had been seasonally cool when Cameron left the rural conference center with other members of the Mindful Writers Retreat group. Dawn had barely broken at that early October hour, but, since then, the air had warmed up considerably. The sun shone brilliantly above the hills, illuminating a rugged wilderness.

Wow, Cameron thought. *Where am I? This doesn't look like western Pennsylvania!*

He fished his cell phone out of his jacket pocket and pressed the Home button. Nothing displayed; a black screen stared back at him. *I just charged it,* he thought with a frown.

He studied his surroundings more fully. Something else seemed off, different. The sky looked a deeper blue, the air felt fresher, more...pristine. Sweat trickled down his back underneath his T-shirt. He doffed his jacket, wishing now he'd worn shorts instead of jeans. Barely able to keep his eyes off the hypnotically beautiful vista, he forced himself to his feet.

How did I get here? he wondered again, more and more confused. *Why can't I remember?* He assumed a path had allowed him access to this high vantage point, but overgrown, waist-high thickets blocked the way behind him.

With a start, Cameron realized he must have wandered away from the well-marked hiking trail. He'd broken the main rule of the Walking Meditation segment of the Mindful Writers Retreat.

Don't wander off the paths.

Dumb ass!

Cameron had been so distracted by his writing project, his thoughts inward, he hadn't really been paying attention. The walking meditation was designed to get the creative juices flowing before breakfast, to help in the writing process when everyone resumed their work. He thought he'd surely get past the block to the book he'd planned to work on this week. But, this morning, just like the previous two, nothing seemed to click.

And now this. Man, the rest of the group would kid him unmercifully. Especially his girlfriend Valerie, who'd joined him at the retreat. All in good fun, he knew, but he still felt foolish.

Crap! He tied his jacket around his waist, took a deep breath, and tried his cell phone again. Hopefully, Valerie would pick up or he'd have to try to contact the conference center staff, who would probably come to rescue (and embarrass) him in one of their goofy golf carts.

If they could even get up here to this spot. Again, nothing displayed on his phone. He couldn't even bring up his GPS app to check his location.

For a moment, the dream or whatever he'd experienced returned. Fragmented and indistinct, strange and confusing, the images were, nevertheless, startling. Gateway to madness? A shaman with snakes for hair? Hiawatha?

A heartbeat of clarity intervened. Just for a moment, Cameron thought he knew what those dream-images meant. Hiawatha. Yes… And then it was gone.

A murmuring drifted through the air, breaking his concentration. A lone voice, soft and whispery, sounded from a distance. *All right!* Cameron pumped a fist in relief. *Either someone else is lost or they've tracked me down.* Even a golf cart would be a relief right now.

He moved toward the direction of the voice. A small path he hadn't noticed cut through the trees and ground cover, running along the ridge. He picked up his pace as the voice grew louder. It sounded like chanting. He was about to call out when another sound reached his ears, rhythmic, insistent.

Cameron stopped, listening. Drum beats? One of the retreat participants played the bagpipes and had performed for the group. But he didn't know of anyone attending the retreat who played the drums.

Again, a chill washed over him.

"You're here. Good. I've come to show you the way."

Cameron jumped. A woman stood on the path, which, a moment before, had been empty. She faced him from a few feet away, her hands held in front of her as if in prayer. Cameron stared.

She wore a deerskin dress and moccasins. Her long hair, styled in a single long braid, trailed down her back. Shell earrings graced her pierced ears, her neck adorned with a matching necklace. She smiled out of a strikingly beautiful, copper-colored face. "*Sekon*, Ayenwatha," she said in both English and Iroquois. "I'm New Face. Welcome."

"*Sekon*, New Face." *Hello*. Cameron returned the Iroquois greeting without a second thought. He was of Mohawk descent and his parents had made certain Cameron and his sister could speak and understand their native tongue as well as snippets of other Indian languages.

Cameron never had much use for those as he got older. Like many Native Americans of his generation, he had immersed himself in the white world and its modern culture. He'd moved to the city after college, got a job in the IT industry, and did very well.

As he entered his thirties, he'd reconnected with his heritage, his family, and tribe. The urge, the passion, to write about his experiences took hold. He started a blog about his upbringing, his life as a young Mohawk living on the St. Regis Reservation in Upstate New York. He'd planned on combining his blog entries into a book, to work on it at the writing retreat.

Am I dreaming all this? he thought. If so, it was the most tactile and lucid dream he'd ever had.

"Come," the woman called New Face said, interrupting his musings. "The Onondaga Prophet awaits. We must be united against the Entangled." She turned and strode down the path. New Face moved gracefully, almost as if she floated rather than walked.

Cameron's breath caught in his throat, his heart thumped in his ears. The same dizziness he'd felt earlier surged over him again. The Onondaga Prophet? The Entangled? And she, New Face, had called him...Ayenwatha?

Again, that flitting spark of knowledge teased him. Cameron knew those designations. He'd researched a lot of Indian history and myth, recorded interviews and conversations with the older members of his family and his tribe. He'd thought at one point he'd use a Mohawk pseudonym for his blog and novel, in order to sound more interesting. Ayenwatha, for no particular reason, had been one of the names he'd considered.

Which was another name for the person in his dream. Hiawatha.

Cameron followed New Face, unable to resist, moving as if he could no longer control his actions. He needed to understand this whole strange experience!

In a few moments, with the drums reverberating through the forest, Cameron and his strange guide arrived at a clearing in the woods. Wide and oval-shaped with the tree line encircling its border, the clearing opened above to a brilliant patch of blue sky. And the sun...

Cameron squinted. The sun. Its bright yellow disc had changed, now appearing as if a small slice had been taken out of the upper right edge of it.

An eclipse, he thought, averting his eyes. *It looks like the start of an eclipse. I don't remember hearing anything about it.*

The chanting emanated from a man standing near the middle of the clearing. He stopped and turned toward Cameron and New Face. Tall, middle-aged and imposing, he radiated an air of nobility and strength. "Ay...Ayenwatha," he said haltingly, as if he had trouble speaking. He wore a long, feathered cloak over a deerskin shirt and pants. His long hair hung loosely past his shoulders. "You...have come."

The Onondaga Prophet.

"We're here to...to confront...the Entangled," the prophet said. "We must forever seal...off the p...portal the Entangled and its sp...spawn will use to enter and violate the Earth."

The Entangled again. The Great Enemy. *My God,* Cameron thought, feeling the first touches of awe and, yes, fear. *This is really happening!* This was no dream. He had become a part of something outside normal experience. Something numinous. He had come to this place and time to take part in a great battle. To join these companions, garbed in another persona.

For New Face and the Onondaga Prophet didn't see him as Cameron Greene, but as Ayenwatha, part of the threesome who would form the Iroquois Confederacy. New Face was Jigonhsasee, the Peace Queen, who would eventually be called the Mother of Nations. The Onondaga Prophet was Deganawida, the Great Peacemaker. And Ayenwatha was Hiawatha, the eloquent orator who spoke for the Peacemaker because of Deganawida's stutter. Together, they would battle against Atotarho, a warrior-shaman whose head sprouted Medusa-like serpents and opposed the peace with his dark magic.

During a total eclipse in the eleven-hundreds!

The drums quieted, their unseen drummers ceasing the pounding cadence. The bordering greenwood rustled and shivered as lithe, shadowy forms appeared. Some possessed hooves, others scales, furred paws, or wings. Bright primal eyes flashed. The creatures of the Earth had come to lend their support, energy, and power to Cameron and his comrades.

The sky darkened, and the air immediately cooled. An aurora of orange light appeared above the tree line as the eclipse entered totality.

At that moment, the space in the middle of the clearing sparked and shimmered. The air seemed to fold in upon itself. It flickered, expanded, splintering into shards of red fire.

An opening coalesced, a huge maw of fiery radiance. The Entangled would enter through that gateway, he who wasn't really a warrior/shaman but something else. Something alien and bestial. A malevolent, star-born entity, who, with its deadly spawn, would invade the Earth and destroy its peoples.

"This is what I've foreseen in my dream-visions," the Onondaga Prophet said, his stutter gone in the face of this impending horror. "We can't oppose the Entangled until the portal opens. Only then will our combined might work against it."

The drumbeats began again, louder, faster, taking on a more urgent rhythm. Cameron stood at New Face's right, the Onondaga Prophet on her left. Cameron, as Ayenwatha, felt no fear now, only a determination, a ferocious willingness to fight back, to stop this abomination that threatened all life.

The Entangled appeared within the red nimbus, massive, horrific. Obscenely manlike, it possessed a bulbous head with wide, lidless, blood-red eyes. Long, slimy tentacles undulated from its demonic, gray-skinned face, neck, and shoulders. Ropey arms reached out, claws glinting from its inhuman hands. A stench of decay and death emanated from it.

It placed a taloned foot on the ground.

Cameron and his companions clasped hands and began to sing. He felt a power surge through him, from and to the others. A power emanating from their mystical cores, their souls, their animas, their life forces, concentrated against the emerging threat.

They sang of hope, of life, of renewal.

The Entangled opened its slit of a mouth and roared, its tentacles flailing. It stretched out an arm, as if to deflect the force directed against it. No doubt it hadn't expected such resistance. It pushed its own foul power against its attackers.

The dark energy lashed out, striking at Cameron's and his comrades' minds, clawing at their confidence, empowering their deepest fears. Teeth clenched, sweat beading on his forehead, Cameron sang louder, stronger, joining his voice to those of his comrades.

The Entangled faltered, cringing, its power crumbling. With a howl of defeat, it lowered its head and fell back into the nimbus. The gateway flashed and closed as white sunlight relit the Earth. The eclipse and the danger had passed.

Cameron realized he clasped New Face's hand in an iron grip. New Face gently disengaged and touched his arm. She smiled, her face as bright as the reborn sun. She hugged him, then turned, and embraced the Onondaga Prophet.

"It's done," the Prophet said. "When the other Indian Nations le...learn of our victory, they'll join us in the New Mind, in our quest for...everlasting peace."

"It won't last," Cameron blurted out, knowing how the future, his people's future, would unfold. "The white world will destroy the Indian Nations and their ways of life."

"We know this," New Face said. "But this moment's victory will, one day, reach into the far future, beyond the Earth to the stars themselves."

The stars? Cameron smiled at the sound of those strange but wondrous words.

"What...we have done here," the Onondaga Prophet said, "will affect tho...those who come after us, those of all races. The New Mind and its great peace...will survive the passing of time and encompass all."

"*Niá:wen*, Ayenwatha," New Face said. *Thank you.* "Now go and tell our story. Write the truth which will enlighten our descendants and the others who join us."

She smiled. "Cameron."

Before he could voice his surprise, the world shrunk to a point of bright blue light far, far away, and Cameron was gone.

***

Niá:wen, Jigonhsasee and Deganawida.

A vibration buzzed against Cameron's hip, startling him into awareness, his thoughts scattering. He leaned against the bole of a large white pine. A sign affixed to the trunk read "Blue Trail." The path Cameron had been walking at the retreat.

Surrounded now by typical Pennsylvania fall foliage, Cameron saw no rocky ridges, felt no summer warmth. He untied his jacket from around his waist and put it on in the chilly air.

One other thing, he thought, a slow smile spreading. No prophets or wise women were here to greet him, and he encountered no...eldritch monsters.

But the white pine struck a chord. That tree had been deemed the "Tree of Peace" by the Iroquois Confederacy.

Cameron answered his phone. "Hey, Cam," Valerie said on the other end. "You okay? We're all here at breakfast. You didn't get lost, did you? I knew we should have walked together!" He heard the stifled laughter in her voice.

Cameron took a couple of deep breaths before answering. Lost? Maybe, but he felt if he'd found something instead, or something had found him. Something epic to help him with his writing, to break the block, and tell a story worth telling, albeit with some creative license. He figured no one would be ready for the whole truth.

At least not yet. He didn't know why he'd experienced that event, why he'd been... *chosen*, or how it all had happened in the first place. But he had, and it did.

"Hey, Val," he answered. "Yeah, I'm okay. Sorry, just got, uh, into the walking and zoned out."

"Yeah, well, you better get back here soon, or your pancakes are mine!"

Cameron laughed. He needed to talk to Val about this "vision" of his, but not yet. He had to put it all down in words first. Writing was his true calling and he had been given his first assignment, a great responsibility.

Taking a deep breath, Cameron headed back to the conference center, suddenly hungry for more than just breakfast.

***

TREE OF PEACE CELEBRATION

Come rejoice with us at the annual commemoration of the founding of the First Native Offworld Settlement. This year our guest-of-honor will be Adalia Greene, descendant of Cameron Greene, who wrote under the name of Ayenwatha Bigtree.

Ms. Greene will read passages from her ancestor's groundbreaking and influential book, *Native American Myth to Future History,* at the Great Earth Migration History Center on Gathering Day during the Moon of the Flowers. A reception will follow.

As always, all are welcome.

LARRY IVKOVICH

Freedom City
Haudenosaunee Home World
Argun-Serae System
C.E. 2358

A LIGHT IN THE WOODS
by Lori M. Jones

Death.

Death is what we all have in common. So, this should be a fun time.

"Please take a seat, Michael. Welcome, campers!" She crooned that greeting. I'd never used the word "crooned" before but I'd never actually heard crooning until I'd met Counselor Kathie. And I now know I don't enjoy crooning.

In the camp's main gathering room, just one open seat remained in the circle, so I had no choice but to sit between a girl with a sparkly headband and a chubby kid with a crewcut. They were both smiling at me like I was a game show host with a microphone.

The crooner continued, "You're all so blessed to share this week with each other. No one understands what you've been through like one another."

Our fathers were murdered, so "blessed" is not what I would call us.

"Let's open in prayer…" The crooner apparently doesn't think God appreciates her crooning, so her voice dipped into a gentle, lullaby-like song.

The whole group said, "Amen," together, out loud, like they'd practiced this show before. I scanned the room, assessing my new *friends* for this stupid week. Besides Chubby Crewcut and Headband, I also named a few more other friends: Narrow Angry Eyes, Pensive Polly (Her real name was really Polly. I kid you not.), Beefy Bob (Robert, he goes by, ROBERT. At least that's what his ALL CAPS nametag said) and Total Hottie.

Total Hottie just made this stupid retreat interesting.

Headband raised her hand to speak, thanked the group, thanked the counselors, and thanked Jesus for this opportunity.

Seriously, Headband? She caught my eye-roll.

"This week," announced the crooner, "we'll do things to honor the parents you've lost in the line of duty, but most importantly, this week's for you! Your feelings! Your time to pray, to laugh, to cry if you want and to learn about yourselves."

Headband raised her hand again, I kid you not.

"The agenda looks amazing! But do we have to participate in all the activities?"

"Yes, we ask that you do. There's a reason for each activity, so we want you to try."

There were going to be a lot of discussions about grief and the death of our fathers. Topics I preferred to keep to myself. So, I agreed with Headband, because I had a feeling she wasn't up for everything planned for this week, too. Although I'm sure Headband would be into sharing. She reminded me of my ex-girlfriend. I knew the type. Let me guess, we'd hear how her perfect upper-middle class suburban life was ruined when her detective dad died and then her mom, who was probably a doctor, suffered emotionally but then remarried Stan from church and life was great again.

The crooner told us about crafts, fellowship, hiking and the ropes course. Headband scrunched her face at the mention of the ropes course, but that's the first time I smiled all morning. Something to look forward to. Ropes course, and possibly talking to Total Hottie.

I heard Headband tell Beefy she had a fear of heights. Headband was cute, don't get me wrong, but I wanted to reach over and mess up her perfect blonde hair. Picturing her dirty in the woods with dead leaves stuck in that hair made me laugh a little. I had to entertain myself, or I would go insane here, for sure. What was next, holding hands and singing around a campfire?

Luckily, it was just time to unpack. My roommate was Beefy Bob. I claimed the top bunk and Beefy took the bottom.

As we each wrestled with bedding, Beefy asked from below, "So when did your dad die?"

The air stopped moving in my lungs. It happens every time I hear the words, *your dad.*

I forced myself to speak to him, hoping it didn't lead to more questions. "A year ago next month. You?"

"Two years ago. It was a car crash. It was a car chase that ended badly."

"That sucks." Of course, I knew how bad it really sucked. Our dads were doing their jobs and died. Regular dads with business jobs didn't have to worry about dying or wearing bulletproof vests or carrying guns and Tasers. Regular dad-jobs didn't require them to carry Narcan in their trunks to help drug addicts.

"What about your dad?" Beefcake asked, tucking his sheets around his mattress. Crazy, right? Like it's a normal, everyday question to ask a kid how his dad croaked. So normal that you don't even need to look him in the eye, but can make your bed like you're asking him his favorite cereal.

"He was shot." I'd never said those words out loud.

"How?"

With a gun, genius.

"Long story." It wasn't but I didn't want to share any more with this stranger especially while making our beds.

Yes, someone was knocking.

"Boys, I have your towels!" It was Crooner.

"I got it," I offered, happy to avoid the awful story I've shared with no one and never would.

***

I sat with Crewcut and Beefy for a semi-decent lunch of hot dogs and mac and cheese, and then we all met in an outdoor chapel, under pine trees that were taller than an office building. There was just enough shade to drown out some of the July sun, but the thick air made us sweat.

While the counselors were getting organized, Headband wormed her way onto the same bench as me.

She brushed the pine needles off the seat before sitting. I inhaled her fruity atmosphere.

Total Hottie was in eyeshot. She pulled at the top of her tank top to billow air up to her flawless face. Very entertaining. And the way her black, silky hair moved together in one giant sheath over her shoulder momentarily hypnotized me.

I must have looked like a weirdo, starring at her hotness for so long, so I shot my eyes upward. In spite of the heat, it was still a pretty cool setting. The majestic trees formed a border around the blue sky. The clouds looked like one brushstroke of white oil paint swooping from the bottom left corner up to the top right. The perfect amount, the perfect balance of colors. I imagined it was my hand that had caused it.

"Hello, campers," barked a fortyish looking guy who had happy eyes compared to his rougher face. His facial scar added a bit of mystery. He only said two words but I already liked him. Unlike Headband, who was dabbing her forehead with the back of her hand.

Happy Scar Face spoke about some rules for being out in the woods, what to do if we get lost, what to do if we see wildlife. I sat a little straighter in my seat. Things got more interesting.

He told us about fisher cats—an animal I'd never heard of—and how one here was unusually large and could be mistaken for a bear cub. When he mentioned bears, Headband let out a little "ooohhh." Part of me liked that she was a bit spooked.

"And there's an albino deer roaming around our property. She's completely white. It's a pretty neat sight, if you're lucky enough to see her." Poor deer didn't even know she was different. "We call her Rudolph since the other deer don't like to play with her." I was sad for Rudolph, but my curiosity was through the roof—or tall pine trees. I had a goal: find Rudolph.

Headband leaned toward me and whispered, "I hear albino deer are good luck." She smiled and nodded like she'd just told me a major secret.

Then Crooner discussed meditation and prayer, and how this lowered our stress, because stress compounds our grief. We read some Bible verses and Crooner said, "Let's bow our heads in prayer."

I didn't. I didn't even close my eyes. I just scanned the tops of people's heads. Everyone was obeying and praying. I didn't want to talk to God.

Dad, can you hear my thoughts? Are you still with me?

The only "prayers" I ever sent up to heaven were to my dad. I wondered if he heard them.

I looked back at the tops of the trees blending in with the sky and my eyes watched a puff of a cloud pass behind them. I inhaled and focused on my breath just like the crooner instructed. It did help. I did feel a bit better. I did it on my own, without a nonexistent God.

"Amen!" the faithful followers sang.

"Ok, everyone," said Happy Scar Face, "let's go explore the woods."

Yes! Finally.

We filed toward a path cut into a wooded area. HSF yelled to us to follow the yellow diamond path.

I tried to catch up to Total Hottie but her strides were surprisingly wide and she navigated the path like a pro. Fearless.

Headband…not so much. Her head was down as if in prayer, her eyes fully focused on every step's landing. She reached for tree trunks for balance. Just then, three deer bolted from our right and dashed across the path ahead of us. All brown deer.

Being surrounded by the trees felt like a giant hug.

Are you seeing this, Dad? Do you know I'm here?

Probably not. He probably didn't hear me, because there was probably nothing after this life. Everyone at this place seemed to believe there was some great God and some great savior who were our amazing friends walking through life with us. But I knew better.

My mind wallowed around that dark place that believed there was no God protecting us, no savior saving us. It felt rebellious to think that so brazenly while surrounded by these robotic believers.

A God would've let us all have a father on this earth. A savior would've saved them from murderers and horrific accidents.

Just then, Total Hottie's stride ceased, and the sound of crunching sticks silenced. We froze. Headband stretched her arm toward the right, while covering her mouth with her opposite hand.

There it was in all its magical splendor.

Rudolph.

***

It was the topic of dinner that evening. How strange it looked and how she appeared almost like a fictional character, like a unicorn. We laughed when Beefy said he nearly screamed like a girl, and Pensive Polly said she peed her pants a bit.

For the first time, I exchanged banter with Headband. We felt bad for the little deer all alone without friends.

She took this as an invitation to go deeper.

"So, how'd your dad die, Michael?" she asked, stabbing a cherry tomato.

"He was shot."

She looked at me like she wanted more, but I refocused on my food. And I didn't ask her anything. I wanted this conversation to end and go back to mystical forest creatures.

Headband shifted her interrogation to others at the table. Pensive Polly shared about how her beat cop dad died—in shocking detail. Right at the end of her story, Crooner asked the room to finish up and return to our rooms for a break and some alone time.

***

We were allowed a few moments of "screen time" during our break and then we were supposed to journal. I opted for no journaling. They had placed a notebook on all of our bunks, but I had tossed it in my suitcase.

Beefy's left arm curled around his notebook, scribbling away with his apparent deep thoughts and feelings. I shook my head at the picture of this big lug of a boy-man all entranced in journal writing.

I grabbed my phone. There were texts from my aunt—the one whose bright idea it was to send me here—checking to see how it was going. And one from my mom, who enjoyed sharing my dad's demise-story as much as I did. She used the "it's a long story" diversion as often as I did.

I answered both texts with the obligatory "Good." And threw in a detail about the food.

My roommate had finished his intense journal entry and was laughing at something on his phone, his beefy thumbs flying around his screen. Just like Headband carried around an atmosphere of fruitiness and sparkles, Beefy's atmosphere was childlike joy. It was annoying.

After visiting the bathroom, Beefy's eyes left his phone and met mine. I knew the look.

"Hey, man, why don't you like to talk about your dad? It's why we're all here and we all get it."

"I don't know. I just don't."

He took a step toward me, with his hands deep inside the pockets on his wide hips.

"I understand. I used to not want to either. For a long time. It hurt too much. But now I find it actually helps the pain to get it out and talk about it."

I sat down on the bed and looked at my phone again to have something to separate me from his piercing blue eye-daggers.

"I just can't." And there it was again, that strangling grip in my throat.

And then he touched my shoulder. I flinched. "Well, if you want to talk, Michael, I'm here." And for a minute I wanted to. I wanted to spill out all the ugly, frustrating details of that night. How he didn't wear his bulletproof vest. How I almost hated him for it. I wanted to tell him about Larry Rocker, the owner of the convenience store, and how I wished he was dead instead of my dad. It was all right there in front of my eyes, like the albino deer, wanting to be in the open, but then he said, "And if you want someone to pray with, I'm here, too." He tapped my shoulder and returned to his bunk.

Prayer. How useless. Prayer couldn't bring my father back. I needed to get out of Beefy's joy-atmosphere.

***

The next morning after breakfast, we gathered in the gigantic pavilion that was completely empty except for some basketball hoops at one end and a stone fireplace on the other. We were divided into teams. My team was Beefy, Headband (ugh) and Total Hottie (yes!). Beefy and Headband would make a cute couple, I thought as their fruity-joyfulness melded together inside our group.

Happy Scar Face explained that we were building a ginormous pyramid. I didn't see how this was possible looking at all the flat pieces scattered around. We first had to build our own four team pieces and then work with the other teams to make it into one big pyramid.

All the different age groups from the entire camp came together for this, so there were a lot of kids. Chaos, too, lots of it. But Happy Scar Face was smiling. I guessed he'd seen this before so it gave me hope that all would turn out okay. I just wanted to be back out in the woods, alone. I wasn't looking forward to talking to my team. Except for Total Hottie.

I tried to get as close to her as possible. Turns out, TH is a bit bossy, but she really knew what she was doing and had a great idea. We assessed each of our skills and TH assigned us tasks. We decided to each do one task on all four tiny pyramids. I got to be the painter, and everyone surprisingly agreed to my theme. White deer. The tiny white deer heads I painted all around our four pyramids looked pretty cool, if I must say so myself.

Another surprise: we assembled our small team pieces with little friction or drama.

Even when we all joined together for the massive construction of the big pyramid, the four of us stuck together. It was actually pretty exciting seeing it all erect into a recognizable structure and it was much bigger than I had imagined. Our white deer pieces got to be the very top, the awarded honor of being the first team to finish. Three of us held a ladder as Headband leaned in to crown the creation. Everyone cheered as we helped her back to the ground.

As I took Headband's hand to help her off the final rung, our eyes connected, and for the first time her– Jenna's–fruitiness didn't bother me.

***

After lunch, the four of us walked toward the woods for a "scavenger hike." Total Hottie said, "Michael, you did a great job on the pyramid project. I didn't think you liked us, but you seemed to enjoy it." Her abruptness was irritating.

"I like you all," I mumbled. Embarrassed. Hot.

"You don't seem to like God very much."

That hurt. As true as it was, that I was angry with Him, it still hurt.

"I suppose you're right. I'm mad."

"He didn't take your dad as a punishment. He's a loving God. The perpetrator caused the harm. And you know, Michael, you can talk to us. That's why we're here."

We were all quiet for a bit, navigating the terrain. TH took the scavenger list from Jenna-Headband, assuming her leadership role again.

We hit our first destination. A worn bench in the clearing.

"It says we need to sit together, face the horizon, and share something the group doesn't know about us."

We sat. TH went first, of course.

"My mom is getting remarried. And although I like James, I'm sad. And mad."

Beefy shared that he was dyslexic.

Jenna said, "I've talked about my mom, so you all assumed it was my dad that was killed in the line of duty. But it was my other mom. I have—had—two moms. They adopted me and my sister."

I had totally pegged her wrong and was still reeling from guilt when they all looked at me to go.

I decided to give them what they wanted, and then maybe they'd leave me alone. I looked up at the sky. Surprisingly, the words rolled out easily. "I'm mad at God, and mad at my dad. He was getting a coffee at the store when he interrupted a robbery. He pulled his gun out, but the robber killed my dad and ran. He was just about to shoot the store owner, but shot my dad instead. I don't know why my dad wasn't wearing his vest. He always wore a vest. I'm mad he didn't shoot fast enough, and I'm mad at God for not stopping it."

"Your dad's a hero," whispered Total Hottie. "He saved that owner's life."

I know. But I wanted my dad's life.

I got up, deciding to move this scavenger hunt along. I didn't want to cry and felt the familiar strangling in my throat.

And then Jenna gasped. We froze. My head had been down and I hadn't seen it until we were right in its path. A black bear. A big one.

Beefy whispered, "Her cub is behind us. We're screwed."

I felt Jenna's hand slip around my arm. She was shaking. So was I.

Our four bodies instinctively slid together to form one structure—like the pyramid. Without saying a word, we all took steps backward, holding on to each other. I wasn't breathing.

The mama bear stopped eating and faced us. I got a whiff of her odor. I reached my arm around Jenna's shoulder and pulled her trembling body close.

Beefy whispered, "Jesus, save us."

My mind raced, trying to remember what to do.

Blank. Nothing, but red burning fear.

With our heads pivoting, we all took another step back. But Mama took two steps toward us, and made a low growl.

"Please, Jesus," TH whispered.

"What do we do?" Beefy breathed.

A loud rustling from behind baby bear caused our collective gasp.

A ghostly figure sprung from the brush. And then disappeared again. It was visible just enough to make out its form.

Rudolph.

It was enough distraction to make the baby run toward its mama, and for Mama to forget about us, and for me to yell, "RUN!"

And we ran.

Ran so fast, I don't think my feet hit the ground once.

We made it back to camp without one of us saying a word.

At the clearing, we gasped, squealed, high-fived, bending over in relief and agony and pure, fruity-joy.

We fell into awkward sweaty hugs, laughing, and Beefy hooted. The cheering helped hide the fact that I was crying a little and I wanted more than anything to kiss Jenna.

***

Later, we gathered in the outdoor chapel for worship. I slid next to Jenna, and Beefy—

Robert—and TH—Wende. We pressed in together, close, just like we had in the woods.

I smiled, and when Crooner—Kathie—asked us to bow our heads, I did.

I thanked God – with my throat constricted—for my new friends. We were like the pyramid, needing each other to lean on, to build on, to absorb pressure and pain.

And maybe God is present everywhere because he's inside each of us, tucked inside our talents, or inside a trembling hand.

Inside Robert's journal.

And inside a white deer.

And inside of a cop buying coffee at a convenience store.

And then I said, along with the rest of the group, "Amen."

LIGHT OF THE MOON
by Ramona DeFelice Long

After three weeks in jail, Mama asked me to talk to Judge Rousseau about getting her some decent food to eat.

"*Mon Dieu,* I am wasting away," Mama said from her cell. Behind her, the narrow cot was covered with a quilt from home, and on top of the wooden crate she used as a table was a kerosene lamp on a doily. She'd left a half played game of solitaire spread over the doily. Where she got playing cards, I didn't know. The Bible that had been on the pillow was nowhere to be seen.

She showed me her bowl of half-eaten stew. I think it was stew. "That old cow Lorraine Badeaux is poisoning me."

"Hush, Mama," I said. "Mrs. Badeaux is doing no such thing."

Mama pressed her face between the bars. Her eyebrows and cheeks lifted up. That, plus the pounds she'd lost eating jail food and all the naps she took out of boredom, made her look as young as me. Trust Mama to turn getting arrested into getting prettier.

"Geneva, *cher*, just go ask him," Mama wheedled. "That sheriff can hardly look at this slop. He passes me my plate and runs away. Or maybe he believes I'll bewitch him, too."

I begged her not to joke about that.

She narrowed her eyes at me. "And *pour l'amour de Dieu*, when you go see the judge, don't wear what you got on. You look like a blind nun dressed you."

"Mama—"

"Your hair's all right, but get you some lipstick and rouge and use it. Judge Rousseau is old, but he ain't dead."

No, he wasn't, but his brother-in-law was, and that's why Mama's bail was set high as the moon. But explaining that to her was like talking to a tree stump.

I said I had to leave. I was Mama's only visitor, and she was bitter. Where was our family? Where were her friends? She was lonely and felt forsaken. I never told her that, at home, nobody came to visit me either, and I had not even murdered anybody.

Most days she begged me to stay, but tonight she told me to get on home. I suppose she thought I had a busy evening ahead tarting myself up before going to see the judge.

***

When the young deputy was on duty, he sat in a chair five feet away from Mama's cell, as if he thought I'd help my mother escape by slipping a bolt cutter under my dress—a dress fit for a convent, indeed, because my teacher contract said I had to "act and keep my person modestly." I worried every day I'd be fired over Mama's scandal.

Sheriff Reyes usually sat in his office up front and read the newspaper. When my visiting time was over, he always asked, "Things all right, Miss Geneva?"

I answered, "Yes, Sheriff, thank you," except for the time or two when Mama asked for a warmer shawl or the quilt off her bed.

Once, horrifyingly, I had to say I needed to come right back; when he frowned, I whispered that Mama needed some womanly things. He let me into her cell with a paper sack that he did not inspect. Had I been wily, I could have slipped her anything—a pistol, liquor, tonic from Madame Velda—but wily was Mama's way, not mine. The sheriff trusted me. If you can't trust a twenty-year-old spinster schoolteacher who dresses as modestly as a nun, you have faith in no one.

Tonight, Sheriff Reyes stood at the window. The kerosene lamp on his desk lit him up from behind: tall, broad-shouldered, brown hair cut short but still wavy. On one of those shoulders was the scar from a shell that blew him out of the sniper's nest he'd sat in for three days, picking off Germans but never giving away his position. I'd read that in the Bossier City newspaper, when he'd come home a hero after the war ended.

He turned around and said, "Your mother's right. Mrs. Badeaux can't cook."

I didn't speak; he was also very handsome.

"I asked Judge Rousseau if the restaurant could feed us. He said the parish could not afford the expense."

The sheriff lived in a small house attached to the jail. Mrs. Badeaux cleaned for him and the priest and a few others in Bayou Rosa because her husband drank and her only son, Bendict, had gone off to fight in Europe, too, but he didn't come home a hero. He died in the trenches in France.

I felt sorry for the sheriff. I knew what it was like when Mama got set on a complaint. He was always polite but he wasn't a talker, and I'd not once seen him smile. I wondered if he was the one who gave Mama the deck of cards.

"I will go to the judge in the morning," I said, embarrassed. If he heard Mama fuss about her meals, he must have heard her words about my clothes and *toilette*, too.

Outside, the town of Bayou Rosa had edged into darkness. It was cool enough not to worry about mosquitoes, but I reminded myself to fix the tear in the screen door. Mama had never done a thing around the house but now that I lived there alone, keeping it up felt like a world of responsibility.

The moon lit my way. I passed the church and the graveyard. The new section of tombs from two years of Spanish flu glowed in the dark. I crossed myself for Grandmere, who'd taken sick one morning a year ago and was dead before midnight.

My satchel was heavy with Mama's change of clothes and books from school. At home, I set it on the rocker and lit the stove, thinking of that awful stew. Growing up, my male relatives came by with food for three women living alone: chicken parts, fresh game, a bucket of shrimp or bushel of oysters, turtle meat and blood sausage and hogshead cheese. After Grandmere died, the offerings slowed down. The flu took some of my cousins, too. Now, nobody in the family would set foot in our tainted house and Madame Velda charged too much to purify it.

I peeled two potatoes and onion and garlic and made a hash. My teacher salary could support one person, but I missed the leftovers Mama carried from her job washing dishes at the restaurant. While my supper cooked, I went out on the back porch, avoiding the spot that got stained with Victor Mayet's blood, and put Mama's clothes and my school dress in a tub to soak.

Bugs swirled around the kerosene lamp I set on the railing. I heard rustling in the blackberry bushes and ferns in the woods that crept closer each season, but the sounds did not frighten me. They reminded me I was not alone in the world.

I leaned against the post. Some nights, my loneliness felt like a living thing. When Mama lived with me, I never knew where she might be—wildcatting who knows where with who knows who—but I did not feel the oppression of just me, just this house, just my single plate and cup on the table. Just my one pillow on the bed.

Overhead, the half-moon was bright in the indigo sky. One of Grandmere's old sayings, "Marry a man by the light of the moon and he will stay true to you," came to me, but I went inside and let the screen door with the rip on the side bang behind me. Moon or no moon, what man would have me now?

***

I woke up early and walked to the jail through a fog clinging to the road, but I didn't visit Mama. During the night, sunk down into my soft moss mattress, an idea came to me. I told it to the sheriff, and a half hour later we were in the judge's kitchen. His wife's mouth had formed a thin line when she saw me, but since Sheriff Reyes was at my side, she did the polite thing and offered us coffee.

I told the judge that I could barter duties with Mrs. Badeaux. I'd provide breakfast and supper every day for Mama and the sheriff, and Mrs. Badeaux would clean the schoolhouse three times a week. I would do this for the two months Mama would be in jail awaiting trial. It was that long before a circuit judge could make his way here. Judge Rousseau had to recuse himself from presiding over Mama's trial since the victim was his brother-in-law.

Two months of free meals for a prisoner and the sheriff. The judge might be old like Mama said, but he knew a good deal when it was presented to him, even without lipstick or rouge.

In front of the schoolhouse, I thanked the sheriff for accompanying me. He removed his hat and his wavy hair sprung up. In the sunshine, he seemed almost as young as me instead of ten years older.

"Miss Geneva, with all this talk about meals, I never did ask if you were a good cook," he said, just about the longest sentence I'd ever heard him speak.

"No, Sheriff, you never did," I said, and turned around and walked through the gate. Later, when we were engaged, he told me that moment was the first time he saw me as anything other than a murderess' daughter.

I could cook. I could sew. I could embroider and do needlepoint and read the Psalms in a pleasant voice. I could play the piano and paint a still life of an apple. I'd been taught all the domestic arts, plus how to be a teacher, at the convent school where Grandmere sent me when I was fifteen. How she got the money for it, I never knew, but I suspected the family got together and pitched in the same way they had pitched in with food. It was not my fault, after all, that my mother had me when she herself was fifteen, or that all through my childhood, she took up with any man who said they'd run away together if she did this or that with him. No man ever did take her away from Bayou Rosa, no matter how many times she did the this or the that. Whoever my daddy was, Mama never said.

I might have got a teaching job in Biloxi or even Memphis, but Grandmere died and Mama begged me to come home. And then, three weeks ago, Victor Mayet—brother of the judge's wife—came round to the back porch and told Mama she had bewitched him. When she laughed, he charged up the steps and pulled her hair and slapped her face, and Mama had no choice but to shoot him with her dead father's .22. That was her story, though her hairdo was in place and she didn't have any mark on her cheek.

"What was I supposed to do?" she said to the lawyer Judge Rousseau arranged to represent her. "Let the man beat up on me?"

The lawyer said, "The problem is, you shot the man in the back and he wasn't wearing any pants." Mama sighed and said, *c'est vrai*. It was not the first time a man not wearing any pants had been a problem for her.

***

I gave my students a test on Ancient Egypt, and while they wrote about pharaohs and pyramids, I planned supper. The nuns had taught me canning, so I had beans and peas and vegetables from last summer, and plenty of rice and onions and garlic. With more time, I could have made a succotash with corn and okra; if I had ham hocks, the meal would be tastier, but I only had what I had. My salary could stretch to buying some andouille or alligator meat, but not every day. I blessed Grandmere, and the nuns, for instructing me how to stretch staples into a hearty meal.

When I got home, a horse was tied to the fence post and the sheriff sat on the front porch holding a burlap sack. He said, "Rabbit. Trapped it this morning." He had more of an upstate accent than a bayou one, I noticed. The old newspaper story said he was a farmer's son and had grown up trapping, hunting, and fishing. He could shoot anything from any distance, and sitting in duck blinds and deer stands had taught him patience.

"*Bien merci*," I said.

He said, "You're welcome."

I held the burlap sack to my stomach. "Sheriff, can I ask you a question?" I didn't wait for him to say yes or no, but added, "Do you think Mama will hang for shooting Victor Mayet?"

He pursed his lips. "I can't tell what a jury will decide."

That was not what I asked. "But what do you *think*?"

He turned his head and squinted like he was following something moving in the woods, or maybe he wasn't used to be asked what he thinks. I asked him because, aside from Mama, he was the only person I could think of who had taken a life.

Still staring at the woods, he said, "It doesn't look good for her."

That was more like an answer, though not the one I wanted to hear.

"Don't tell her," I said. "About the meal, I mean," as if he might go to the jail and discuss Mama's chances with the jury with her.

He tipped his hat at me, mounted his horse, and rode off.

That night, Mama nearly wept when I surprised her with rabbit sauce picante and hot rice and stewed green beans. I sat with her while she ate, but my mind was in the other room, wondering if my cooking was to Sheriff Reyes's liking. Mama chattered while she ate, and when it was time to go, she said, "*Merci, cher,* that was good as

Grandmere's," which was the highest compliment she could give.

The sheriff gave me something better. When I carried in Mama's dishes—the plate licked clean—he took the tray from me, and smiled.

***

I cooked shrimp boulettes, turtle soup, okra gumbo, pork stew, jambalaya, and *grillades*; I baked corn bread and *pain perdu*, and fried catfish for dinner and apple fritters for breakfast. Every day or so, the sheriff brought me some fresh kill. One Saturday morning, he appeared with a small live chicken. He'd been up late breaking up the Friday payday fights, so he hadn't had time to wring it. He did that out of my sight and plucked it on the back porch, over the spot where I'd spent hours on my hands and knees scrubbing out Victor Mayet's blood. The chicken fricassee I cooked that day was the best I'd ever eaten.

The days got shorter and the sheriff took to walking me home. A single woman alone on the dark street was risqué; a single woman and a single man walking together usually caused gossip, but no one questioned Sheriff Reyes. Escorting me home safely was only him performing his job, but his willingness to be seen in public with me made me feel less tainted.

One night, after a supper of roasted *poule d'eau*, we walked in silence as usual, but after I wished the sheriff a *bon nuit*, he said, "Don't you think it's about time you called me Emile?"

I said, "Is it?" Mama had been in jail six weeks and I had seen him every day since I started cooking for them, but I knew no more about him than I knew from that newspaper article, and though he complimented my meals and inquired after my mother's well-being, he never once asked a question of me, or about me.

He stepped closer and removed his hat. Behind his head was the moon, round and yellow like a halo. Nothing at the convent school had prepared me for a moment like this. I said, "Why are you so kind to me?"

Sheriff Reyes took my hand. His was big and hard; mine felt like a child's in it.

"It's not kindness, Geneva," he said. "Don't you understand that I've been courting you?"

Well, no. I never understood that one little bit.

***

"You sly dog," Mama said when I told her the sheriff—Emile—and I would be getting married. Then she called, "Sheriff! Sheriff! Come back here!" before I could quiet her.

He rushed in like the place was on fire, but all she did was stand with her hands on her hips, curvy again from good eating, and said, "Don't you have something to ask me?"

He blinked at her. I hissed, "Mama!" but she shushed me.

"If you want to be marrying my daughter, you got to do things proper," she told him. "You got to ask for her hand from me."

My face flushed with chagrin, but Emile laughed—a man's deep laugh that shook his body and echoed off the walls of my mother's jail cell.

I had made him smile, but it was Mama who got a laugh out of him.

We chose a spot in the woods for the wedding, a clearing near the bayou where Grandmere and her husband had exchanged their vows. It was Mama's idea, and Emile agreed; when she begged to see her only child get married, he and I went to see the judge again. Judge Rousseau said Mama could attend if Emile himself escorted her to and from the jail. The judge trusted no one else.

I bought a length of dark blue cotton and sewed myself a wedding dress. The school board said I had to quit at the end of the year because a married woman could not be a teacher, but that was all right with me. Emile would live at my house, and I could practice all my domestic arts and womanly skills on him, and no matter if Mama was spared or hanged, I would not be alone anymore.

The evening of my wedding, I put on my dress and a lace collar that had been Grandmere's. The judge arrived at dusk and brought two of my cousins as witnesses. Fireflies danced among the blackberry bushes, and we walked on a rough path into the woods. At the clearing, the judge hung a lamp from a tree branch and Henri, who brought along a fiddle, began to play it. Henri played while we waited for Mama and Emile. He played while the judge began checking his pocket watch. He played while a feeling like a hard knot of pine grew in my stomach. Finally, when Henri ran out of songs to play and Emile's horse never appeared, the judge said, "You know something you need to tell me about, Geneva?"

I was almost too stricken to speak. I swallowed and said, "No, Judge, I do not."

Henri and his brother ran back to town. They returned, and I stood in my blue dress and lace collar and listened to Henri say the jail was empty and Emile's horse was gone and all his belongings in the sheriff's house were missing, and all that was left in Mama's cell was a deck of cards.

***

I got to keep my teacher job. Every few weeks, the young deputy comes by to ask if I've heard anything from the fugitives. He doesn't bring anything to cook, though he is the temporary sheriff now and lives in the house next to the jail and has to endure Mrs. Badeaux's meals. I tell him truthfully that I never heard a word, and that I never expect to.

At night, sometimes, when the moon is full, I go outside and stand on the spot where a man's blood seeped into our porch while he lay there dying. I face the woods and recall the sound of the fiddle on what should have been my wedding day, and I wonder what moment, exactly, was the one when Mama had bewitched him. She'd had no lipstick or rouge, her dress was plain and she couldn't cook, so maybe she offered the sheriff a this or a that, and in that jail cell where I'd brought her a quilt and a shawl and home-cooked meals, Sheriff Reyes took it.

That's what folks in town say, but I do not want to think that way. It makes her look bad, and him, too, so I think instead that Emile did what every other man had promised, but no other man ever did. He took Mama away from Bayou Rosa, and saved her from hanging, and all that had to be bartered in exchange for that was me.

LINGERING MEMORY
by MaryAlice Meli

My screaming woke my mother. And not for the first time. I told her spiders were in my bed again. She whispered, "Be quiet, Charlotte. Your father and baby brother are sleeping." Then, she grabbed the book of nursery rhymes she had been reading to me and guided me down two flights of stairs to the cellar.

Still holding my hand, she led me through the dark basement to the giant, round, metal furnace and opened the door. Heat from the roaring blaze flooded my face.

My mother held my hand but let go long enough to tear a page from my book, the page that had a fat, black, leggy spider on it next to Miss Muffet's tuffet. The picture showed Miss Muffet running away. I squeezed my eyes shut and tried to hide my face in my mother's bathrobe but she wouldn't let me. She smoothed the page against the book and turned my face to the images and said, "Look, Charlotte! Look at the page!" When I opened my eyes, she held the page to the edge of the fire. As the edges curled and devoured the spider, she threw the whole page inside, turning the escaping Miss Muffet and the whole page black.

My mother slammed the door of the furnace and said, "Now the spider is gone. All gone."

I reached for mother to lift me into her arms but she told me I was too big to pick up anymore. She walked me back to my room. She tucked me under my covers and said, "Go to sleep now. You won't see the spider anymore, will you?"

I shook my head but couldn't say the word no because I knew something my mother couldn't know. I'd seen the spider move on the page toward the little girl who had dark hair just like mine. I hoped Miss Muffet got away. I didn't remember the dream about it; I just remembered feeling more scared than I'd ever been in my five years.

After that, things happened on pages I was reading in class that other children didn't see. Not as I did. Like the leaping troll under the bridge or the gulping killer whales in the sea. I saw them move. I'd look quickly around the classroom but most students were calm, one or two sleeping. I asked my friends if they noticed the troll jumping up and down as though he was about to burst through the veil of the page.

They laughed and said, "You're crazy, Lottie!"

I laughed, too, and said, "Just kidding." I knew then I could never tell anyone what I saw if that's what my friends thought. Mother might take me back to that doctor who tried to convince me that what I saw was my active, childish imagination. Finally, I agreed with him to be pronounced cured so Mother would take me home.

I was able to keep my secrets throughout the rest of my school years. That changed in college, the images seemed stronger than those I saw when I was younger. The veil between their world and mine seemed thinner. On the various pages, a claw pressed its sharp point nearly through the page. I wrinkled my nose at the stink of leaf rot from a pond and heard distant scratching and growling. Was it because I was older that the images and sensations seemed that much stronger?

I was able to balance my life evenly until the day of the field trip in botany class.

We gathered on the wide campus green. Our professor was explaining that we were to draw as many plant specimens listed in the assignment as we could find. He said that because rain was starting, we could take phone photos instead and make the drawings later. The professor reminded us to search carefully as the plants were concealed under larger growth in the forest.

As we spread out and moved toward the forest where the plants were, the trees seemed to be coming forward as though to meet me. I felt dizzy with the movements. I closed my eyes and waited until I'd regained my balance. The students' chatter brought me back to the assignment. I followed a group where everyone seemed to be taking photos.

"Over here," a guy named Tim shouted. "There's a ton of different plants."

We shuffled through the damp weeds to join him. I looked where he was pointing. A huge spider web seemed to encase an entire shrub.

"Don't worry about this guy." Tim pointed to the web, breaking half of it when he pushed the shrubbery back to reveal the plants we needed to photograph. "I'll hold it back for you." I was the last one in line to photograph the plants. As I focused on the delicate stems, Tim let go of the shrubbery and it whipped back over the plants. A fat globe with a head and enormous long, black legs perched at a web hole in the center.

I froze. I couldn't speak. I was barely breathing.

"Oww. What the hell…" Tim, shaking his hand, looked at me. "I'm sorry. I didn't let go on purpose. Something pushed the shrub forward. Scratched the crap out of my hand. Are you okay?"

I couldn't take my eyes off the hideous arachnid, swaying on the slowly steadying shrub. Tim saw what I was staring at and whistled low and long.

"Whoa, I don't think we want to disturb Bubba anymore." He took my arm and walked me back to the green. "I know spiders grow big but not in cities in the cold northeast."

"I'm never coming back here. I don't care if I fail the assignment."

"Give me your email address and I'll send you the photos I took."

I felt relieved. "Thanks. I'm Charlotte." I put out my hand.

He laughed. "Like *Charlotte's Web*?"

LINGERING MEMORY

I nodded. The trees behind him were advancing.

WALKING THE PLANK
by Gail Oare

"Walk the plank! Jump! Jump!"

Jimmy took the leap. When he hit the sea, he began treading for his life, surrounded by jagged sharks' teeth.

Okay, they weren't teeth—only blades of tall grass, but to us they were a frenzy of hungry creatures, deadly predators in the ditch beneath the bridge. Jimmy shrieked and giggled as the grass snapped at him in the warm breeze.

"Alright, Jimmy," Norma shouted as she walked toward the path. "Let's get going."

The sun was merciless that June morning, so we were headed into the woods at the end of our street to find some shade. But first we had to cross the narrow footbridge— the plank of our pirate ship—stretching over the ditch at the entrance to the path. All the kids in the neighborhood knew about this plank made of two two-by-fours side by side, and at one time or another each of us was forced to walk it. The entrance to the woods across the bridge was a natural gathering place, and we'd regularly meet up and play with whomever we found loitering there. School had been out for the summer since early June, and we had two more full months with nothing better to do than board the pirate ship and disembark on the "island" to search for buried treasure. This was our domain, and no one could take it away from us.

On this particular day, the plank of our pirate ship was manned by my older sister Norma, who was ten years old, my best friend Carrie, Jimmy, who lived next door to Carrie, and me.

The youngest of the group was required to walk to the edge of the plank and jump. On that day it was Jimmy, otherwise it would have been Carrie or me. I admit that I felt a little disappointed not being the one to be sacrificed, the one chosen to leap into the air and feel the chill along my spine from the cool tickle of the grass.

But there was no way around it. Rules are rules, and when it's your time, it's your time. Only after the designated kid walked the plank could we move on to play along the path.

"Come on, Jimmy," Norma shouted again. "Hurry up."

Jimmy flailed his arms with all the silliness of a typical five-year-old before he turned toward the embankment. His pink hands clawed the earth and his legs splayed like a frog as he found purchase on the rocks. Then with a single leap he was out of the ditch and out of the sea.

He caught up to us as we entered the mottled shade of the ash grove. Of course, we were the good pirates and the trees were really palm trees on the island where we had landed. It wasn't even noon yet, and the sun was harsh and the air heavy. We really did feel like we were crossing a tropical island.

The three of us walked along slowly in the heat but Jimmy kept running ahead, eager to get to wherever we might be going. "What's your rush, Jimmy?" Norma kept saying. "Slow down. Stay where we can see you." Jimmy would laugh and slow for a little bit but then take off again.

Eventually we reached the point where the path split in two. The left branch was well worn, but the right one was overgrown with ivy and briars. We'd never taken the right path before, and on this day we decided to explore it.

Thorns scratched at our arms and snagged our T-shirts as we moved through the overgrowth. The path rose gradually along a hillside, but as we neared the crest it abruptly became steeper. Embedded stones gave us footing as we neared the summit. Only then did we feel the soft wave of cool air and hear the splash of water. We walked along the ridge toward the sound until we saw the waterfall. Rushing water from a rocky stream was shooting off the ledge at the top of the falls and splashing off rocks and tree roots into the deep green of a ravine below. A thin mist from the falling water hovered over the moss and ferns along the bank. We had no idea until that moment that the waterfall was here. We were delighted.

We sat on the upper overhang and traced the stream as it emerged from its source at the east side of the ridge, danced along the ridge and dove off the falls. Soon we were tossing pebbles and twigs into the rushing water and watching them tumble haphazardly down the water, bounce off the rocks, and float weightlessly in the air before falling again on their voyage into the abyss beyond our view.

What a find! An ideal pirate hangout. A perfect spot to hide our treasure or find one. "This is *our* place," Carrie declared. "We can't tell anyone else about it!" We all agreed.

We might have lounged on the rocks all day, but something caught my sister's attention. She walked over to the line of trees and squatted for a closer look. "Aw! A baby bird," she said. We rushed over to see for ourselves. Its lifeless body, pink and featherless, lay stretched across a stone beneath a scrawny sapling. The purple orbs of its closed eyes seemed to fill the tiny head. We stared at it. We were fascinated and appalled.

"Poor thing," said Carrie. "It's not fair."

At that moment, I couldn't look at my friend. I knew there would be a couple of tears running down her freckled face, and I didn't want my eyes to water up, too. I agreed with her. We felt sad for the little bird and powerless. We wished we could have found it earlier and put it back in its nest safe from harm. But we hadn't. We couldn't turn back time.

"We'll have to give this little bird a funeral," my sister said decisively, and we all agreed.

"Jimmy and I'll find a burial spot," I said, and away the two of us went. Norma and Carrie turned their attention to preparing the corpse. They gently scooped the tiny bird onto a large oak leaf and began to wrap it mummy-like, cushioning it with grass and ferns. Jimmy and I found a soft mossy mound overlooking the waterfall and dug a hole with a couple of flat-edged stones. With all the gravity and ceremony of a high priestess, my sister carried the bird over to the burial site and laid it down. We covered the tiny thing with earth and replaced the moss, and Carrie laid a small bouquet of wildflowers on top.

"Now, we each need to say something," my sister said. "I'll start." She cleared her throat.

"Here lies Polly, our good and loyal friend."

"With the beautifulest feathers," Jimmy added.

Then it was my turn. "For fifty years, she stood guard at the top mast of our ship to ward off danger."

"Until today," Carrie said. "When she sounded her final warning and died a hero as we fought off Captain Hook and his evil pirates."

Jimmy stared wide-eyed at Carrie as he listened to the story. "Wow," he whispered.

Carrie smiled briefly at Jimmy's wonderment, and then returned her solemn gaze to the small grave.

"And that is why we are gathered here today," my sister continued. "To honor her and to proclaim that this place be called forevermore Polly's Mountain."

We clapped our hands in approval then fell silent again. We couldn't help but feel a little better about the tiny bird after anointing her brief life with special purpose, even if it was only make-believe. I also found comfort in the other part of our story—the part where we survived the dangerous pirates who threatened our adventure in this special place.

We stood a while longer at the gravesite, listening to the water tumble like a recessional down the rocks into the dark ravine below, and didn't notice the sky clouding over until we felt a sudden gust of wind. At the first clap of thunder, we headed for the edge of the ridge and began scurrying through the brush down the hill.

"Remember," Norma shouted from up ahead. "Don't tell anyone what we found."

By the time we reached the main path, the rain was stabbing our backs like knives and we began running toward the road. I kept wiping my rain-soaked hair from my eyes as I scoured the horizon for the bridge. A tip of a plank emerged through the haze just as a sharp clap of thunder struck nearby. We shrieked from fright and raced even faster toward the bridge. We three older kids reached it at the same time, only to see that the embankment had collapsed and the boards were pointing downward. We turned and jumped across the ditch toward the street.

I looked around for Jimmy and saw him running out from under the bending branches in the ash grove. A gray sheet of rain filled the space behind him, obscuring the path like an impenetrable slate wall. He was heading toward the bridge. He must have seen it was gone because he suddenly veered to the left. At the edge of the ditch, mustering all his strength, he took one giant leap. With his little legs stretching out, he soared above the abyss, over the sea of grass, and landed on his knees in the mud on our side of the bank. He rose up and stumbled out onto the street. Then he turned and ran as fast as he could toward home. In an instant, he was out of sight with Carrie not far behind.

Norma and I raced in the opposite direction toward our house as the rain continued to batter down from the black clouds and ricochet up from the pavement. By the time we reached our front gate, my heels were blistered from the rubbing of my rain-soaked sneakers. Then just as abruptly as it arrived, the storm slowed to a drizzle. I could hear the rain pulse along Dad's new metal gutter over the porch. The rushing water overflowed and spilled to the ground as it reached the constriction of the overloaded downspout. The torrent flowing out the bottom of the spout had already gouged out a pool in our side yard where the accumulating water, with no other place to go, swirled in a murky circle. Norma and I stood on the porch steps wringing out our hair.

I looked up the road toward the bridge. Although it was too far away to see, I knew the broken boards were still lying there. But it didn't matter. If we ever were to go back to visit Polly, I thought, we'd still be able to get over the ditch. Even Jimmy could do it.

Norma and I were still catching our breath when the landscape around us—the grass, trees, houses and sidewalk—began to glow silver and gold. I stepped off the porch and headed toward the side yard.

"Where are you going?" Norma asked.

"Nowhere special," I said. I found a stick and jabbed at the side of the muddy pool until I breached it. Ripples of dark water fanned out over the lawn. I stood up and looked toward the street. Every rooftop angle and every drooping leaf was shedding heavy droplets of water that sparkled under the midday sun pushing and pushing through the spent clouds.

THE LAST FAMILY VACATION
by Kim Pierson

I'd just finished medical school when I learned my father had died and left me the Eighty. I hadn't even known he was sick. It had been years since we'd spoken.

And as for the Eighty itself, the last time—the only time—I'd seen the place was the summer before seventh grade. Mom snorted when Dad called the trip he'd planned a vacation, but Maddie and I didn't care. We'd never been on a vacation before, and we'd never been to northern Wisconsin where Dad had grown up.

"We'll have dinner at Cacciatore's, right?" Maddie asked right away, and even Mom smiled then, because the story of how she and Dad had met there was one she'd told us a million times.

"'Course we will." Dad reached down to ruffle Maddie's dirty blonde hair. Maddie was eight, with a talent for knowing what to say to make everything okay. Despite being older, I tended to have the opposite effect.

I was a good helper, though, or so Dad said as we wedged our luggage into the back of our 1979 station wagon, then tied to the roof the two bags that wouldn't fit inside. Mom frowned when she saw our hard work.

"What if it rains, Charlie? Everything will be soaked."

"Now don't you worry about that. I checked the forecast and it's going to be clear all week."

Mom shook her head, but Dad grabbed her hands and danced her around the driveway. "It'll be an adventure," he told her. "We could use a bit of adventure, don't you think?"

Mom surprised me by actually laughing as she shook him off. "The neighbors will think we're nuts," she said, but she was still smiling.

We left at lunchtime, and weren't even out of the driveway before Maddie was asking Dad to tell us more about the property, land we'd only last month learned had been willed to him by an uncle Maddie and I had never met.

"Not much to tell, sweetcake," he said. "It's eighty acres of scrub land on the outskirts of town. It wasn't good for much back when I was a kid, but maybe it's better now. My father made me help Uncle John plant trees all through it one summer when I was younger."

"Are we going to sell it?" I asked.

My parents exchanged glances.

"We might sell the timber and replant," my dad hedged. "Lots of paper mills in that area. Or maybe, if the town has spread enough, someone will want to buy it to build houses there."

"Maybe *we* could build a house there!" I said.

110

"Our jobs are here, Carrie." Mom sounded exasperated. "We can't just pick up and move four hours north."

Dad's eyes twinkled at me in the rearview mirror, though, and I knew he'd considered it too.

We were almost to the Holiday Inn—one with a Holidome where we would actually get to swim—when it began to drizzle, then downpour. Mom didn't say anything, but I knew from the way her mouth pursed together that she was thinking of the suitcases strapped to the roof.

After we checked in and Dad unloaded the luggage, he took Maddie and me down to the pool while Mom began unpacking—draping the wet stuff over the shower curtain rod, the lamp, any place she could find.

"Is Mom coming down, after she's done?" Maddie asked as she stuck her big toe in the water.

I jumped in the pool then, to avoid hearing Dad tell her no.

"It's warm, Maddie, come on in!" I called, surfacing, and in a minute we were all in—doing somersaults, going down the slide, Dad tossing us in the air. I think we all forgot about Mom until Maddie started to cough.

Dad and I both froze at the sound. Maddie had been born with something wrong with her lungs, and her coughing could turn into wheezing and worse. Dad plastered a smile on his face, though. Stressing out about it only made Maddie cough harder.

"You girls wore me out. Why don't we head back to the room and get ready for dinner? I bet I can talk your mom into letting you have dessert tonight, seeing as how it's vacation and all," he added with a wink.

Maddie stopped coughing long enough to climb out of the pool and dry herself off with a thin white pool towel. But then she started up again, and all I could think of was getting her to Mom, who had Maddie's medicine and knew how to handle it when she got sick.

Mom must have had some sixth sense that something was wrong because she had the door open and was looking out into the hallway as we approached.

She hurried Maddie into the room. "What happened?"

"Nothing," I said. "We were in the pool and she started coughing."

"I was asking your father."

Dad sighed. "Carrie just told you."

Mom gave Maddie her medicine and her coughing slowed, then stopped. The room was quiet.

"This is your fault, Charlie," Mom hissed into the stillness. "You and that rain you promised we wouldn't get."

"I wasn't out in the rain," Maddie protested weakly.

"Your suitcase was," Mom said. "And now you don't have anything dry to wear. You'll get pneumonia, and we're four hours from your doctor." Already worked up, her words came out in a staccato rat-a-tat-tat, agitated despite the fact that Maddie's breathing was practically back to normal.

"Mom, I'm fine," Maddie said, at the same time that I said, "She can wear some of my clothes."

Mom whirled around to me, her face blotchy. "Don't think I didn't notice that. That your things stayed dry."

Dad pounded his fist on the bedside table.

"Enough. That's absolutely enough. I was the one who decided what got packed where. Me."

Maddie was crying and I was trying to get her to put on my fuzzy pink pajamas and neither of us saw our mother walk out the door, slamming it for good measure.

By the time Mom returned a few hours later, we were all in our pjs and had eaten our way through the pizzas Dad had ordered. No dessert.

She went straight to Maddie and tried to smooth her hair. "How are you feeling, sweetie?"

Maddie looked at me and squirmed away from Mom's hand. "Fine."

"Did you save any of that pizza?" Mom asked, looking at the boxes. My shoulders tensed as Dad shook his head, but Mom only sighed.

"I tried going to Cacciatore's. It's closed. Been closed ten years now."

She and my father exchanged looks, and Maddie said sleepily, "Before I was even born."

"I'm not that hungry, anyway," Mom said. She settled into bed with Dad, although she didn't kiss him good night.

When morning came, Maddie's clothes were dry enough that Mom let her join us at the restaurant for breakfast. She would not, however, no matter how much Maddie pleaded, allow her to go see the Eighty.

"That's an 'absolutely not,' missy," she said. "It's damp out there, and who knows how much walking is involved? Nope, the three of us will sit here until your father finishes up his business, sells that piece of property, and comes back to drive us home."

"What?" I said. "Why don't I get to go?"

"I need you here to entertain your sister."

"I don't need to be entertained," Maddie complained. "I need Carrie to be able to go so she can tell me what it's like."

"Your father can do that."

"Not the way Carrie can."

"I'll need Carrie's help today," Dad finally said, setting Maddie up for her favorite joke.

"What do you need her help with?" she asked. "Carrie-ing things?"

The two of them laughed hysterically, and I knew I'd won.

"I'll tell you every last detail, just as soon as I get back," I whispered to her before I left.

The Eighty was about fifteen minutes from the Holiday Inn, but it took us longer than that to find it. The woods all looked the same to me, and I don't think even Dad was sure we were in the right place until he saw the brown pickup truck parked along the road.

"You Jim?" he called through the open window to the bearded man sitting within.

"Yep," the man said.

Dad parked the station wagon and we walked back to the truck. "I'm Charles Anderson," he said. "Thanks for agreeing to meet us. John was my uncle. The lawyer said to contact you about the property."

"Yep. I got the forty across the way there." He gestured to the other side of the road. "Kept an eye on your uncle's land for him."

"Ah, well, thanks for that. Say, tell me—you ever get people looking to buy property out here?"

Jim shook his head. "Not many."

"But some?" Dad sounded hopeful.

"Not any," Jim amended.

Dad shrugged, like it wasn't important. "We'll just wander around then. Check out the trees. I helped John plant them, you know."

"You don't say?" Jim had already started his truck.

"Come take a look, kiddo," Dad said, stepping onto the property. "These trees here, the ones in the rows, are some of the ones I planted. Red pine."

He kept on talking, but I lagged behind, running my hand over the rough trunks of the trees I passed. I'd never been in a forest like this one, with trees all lined up like headstones in a cemetery. Pine needles cushioned my steps, and other than my father's nervous commentary, the woods were as silent as a Robert Frost poem.

We walked about ten minutes—long enough for me to start wishing I'd had the sense to drop breadcrumbs because I wasn't sure we'd be able to find our way back to the car. Then, at the edge of a clearing, Dad stopped suddenly. "This isn't supposed to be here."

In front of us was a small wooden house.

Gleaming a freshly-cut-pine yellow, the house seemed to shine in the sun even though the woods that surrounded it were dark. It had a little front porch, and the area under the roof was decorated with all kinds of intricately carved wooden latticework and curlicues.

I peered around one side of it, then the other. The clearing appeared to form a perfect circle around the house.

Dad marched right into it.

"Wait!" I called out, but he was already up onto the porch.

"This is my property," I heard him saying under his breath, as if rehearsing.

I hesitated one second more before following him.

He knocked on the door, then reached for the brass doorknob.

"Dad," I said. "I don't think this is a good idea."

"They cut down my trees. Who knows how long they've been here?" he said, more to himself than me.

"The house looks brand-new, Dad," I said, pulling pathetically at his arm, although I realized as I said it that the doorknob did look pretty worn.

He shook me off, and pushed open the door.

Inside was one large room, flooded with sunlight from the windows that lined the rear wall and those flanking the fireplace to the right. In front of the fireplace was a large wooden table and chairs. To the left was a staircase and an old-fashioned spinning wheel, the kind Maddie and I had seen on our last visit to Old World Wisconsin.

"Looks like we just missed whoever's been living here," Dad said grimly, walking toward the fireplace. "The fire's not completely out. And there's oatmeal in the pot." He stuck his finger in the cast-iron pot that hung on an arm over the coals. "Still warm. They must have run off when they heard us coming."

It should have made me nervous, but it didn't. I trailed behind him, examining everything. I couldn't help but like the tidy little house, and I knew Maddie would love it. It looked like something right out of a storybook.

Three ceramic bowls, each a different color, were stacked haphazardly on a wooden shelf over the fireplace. A single apple sat next to them, too red to be real. A light blue cushion with daisies was tied to the seat of one of the chairs. There wasn't much else to see. I started to cross the room to inspect the spinning wheel, but Dad stopped me.

"It's time we head back. I'm going to have to call the cops about this," he said, his voice rich with disgust.

"Do you have to? Can't we just leave it?" I pleaded. "Whoever's staying here isn't harming anything. Maybe Uncle John even gave his permission to build it."

"Sweetie, John was a very old man when he died. He hadn't been to the Eighty in years. I'm *positive* he had no idea this was here." He paused at the door, where an old-fashioned brass key was sticking out from the inside lock. "It's strange that Jim didn't notice, though."

The sun was still shining in the clearing as we left, but the woods were darker, and we got lost twice on our way out.

"Must be a storm coming," Dad said, looking uneasily at the sky. He seemed as glad to climb inside the station wagon as I was.

Back at the Holiday Inn, Dad launched right into the story of the crazy little house in the woods.

"You wouldn't believe it, Carol, it was this tiny house, all fitted out with ornate gingerbread—" he began, but Maddie cut him off.

"Gingerbread?" she said, her eyes like saucers. "You found an honest-to-goodness gingerbread house in the woods? Like in *Hansel and Gretel*?"

And even though Mom hurried to explain that "gingerbread" here was simply a way of talking about the decorative carving near the roof, Maddie became more convinced with every detail that the house was straight out of a fairy story—if not *Hansel and Gretel*, then *Goldilocks*, or *Snow White*. I could tell Mom was getting ticked and hoped Dad wouldn't mention the spinning wheel, but he blundered on ahead. So Maddie amended her list to include *Sleeping Beauty*. Or possibly *Rumpelstiltskin*.

"Charlie, can we talk for a second? Out in the hallway?" Mom finally said, and I think that was the first Dad noticed how flushed Maddie's cheeks were and how shallowly she was breathing. He looked sheepish as he followed Mom out the door.

I don't know why they bothered to leave. The walls were thin and Maddie and I sat together on the edge of the bed, listening to every word.

"Why in the world would you make up a story like that? Can't you see how overexcited she is, and how it's affecting her breathing?" Mom asked. "She was upset enough about having to miss seeing the place—"

"I didn't make it up," Dad said shortly. "Now if you're finished, I'm going to the police station. Someone's been living on my property."

When Mom spoke next her voice was quiet. "There really is a house?"

"Jesus. Of course there's a house."

Mom's response was muffled, as if they were hugging, or even kissing, and when they came back into the room, the storm had passed.

When Dad returned from the police station, we all drank root beer and played cribbage, penny a point, until past my bedtime. I won enough to buy a pack of Reese's cups from the vending machine, one cup for Maddie and one for me. And for those few hours, the trip was everything I'd always imagined a family vacation would be.

The next morning, though, Mom was cranky and Dad was tired and packing to go home was way harder since Mom said no putting anything on the car top. The only good news was that the police had insisted we meet them at the Eighty before we left: one final chance to see the house. Maddie had even worn Mom down enough to be allowed to come.

When we arrived, the three of us skipped on ahead while Dad waited for the police. He was sure I could find the house on my own, and I was too.

We made our way deeper into the forest. Mom looked nervous, but I knew exactly where to go. I didn't hesitate once—until we got to the clearing, and the house wasn't there. Not one stick of it. The sun still shone into the center like a spotlight, but the star of the show was missing.

I whirled around to my mom and sister, my mouth hanging open.

"It was here yesterday, I swear it!"

"Carrie Ann, it's physically impossible to dismantle and move a whole house in less than twenty-four hours. Impossible." Mom was glaring daggers at me, but I couldn't even care.

What had happened to the house?

"Magic," Maddie breathed, then coughed, only a little, but enough for Mom to start patting at her pockets.

"Maddie's medicine. I must have left it in the car. Stay with your sister."

"You'll be able to find your way back?"

"Of course I will." She turned to Maddie. "I'll hurry, okay?"

Maddie managed a nod. With a hard look at me, Mom left the clearing, walking at first, then breaking into a run. Maddie and I sank to the ground right where we stood.

"There really was a house, right?" Maddie looked up at me with those big eyes of hers.

"Really and truly," I told her. "But don't talk. Rest."

She leaned against me and I put an arm around her, holding her more tightly every time she coughed. And I thought about magic, and how my little sister had to be right about this place, and that if I had a magic wish, the only thing I'd ask for, the only thing I'd ever really wanted, was for Maddie's lungs to be better.

And so I made that wish, silently, my sister in my arms. And I told the fairies, or witches, or whatever magical beings had caused that house to appear and then disappear that if they only granted that one wish, I'd do everything I could to make sure my dad didn't sell this property or cut down their trees—that we'd go away and leave them alone.

I shifted to get more comfortable, and that's when I felt something solid and warm under my hand. Something that hadn't been there when I first sat down.

I pulled it from the grass and held it up to the sunlight.

"Is that the key? The one from the magic house?" Maddie's eyes were bigger than ever.

I managed to look away from the gleaming brass key long enough to tell her that it was. "But it's a secret, Mads, okay? Even from Mom and Dad. I made a deal with the fairies and this is our contract."

She nodded solemnly. "Can you tell me about the deal?" she whispered.

I considered, then shook my head. "How are you feeling?"

"Better," she said, but she coughed a bit.

I could hear the sound of approaching footsteps and raised voices, and slipped the key into my pocket just as two police officers burst into the clearing. Mom was right behind, with Maddie's medicine, and Dad saying over and over that there'd been a house here yesterday. Mom waited until she realized Maddie was okay to start calling him a liar.

I could have pulled out the key right then, proved that Dad and I had been telling the truth. But I'd made a deal. Whatever was here wanted to be left alone, and for that to happen, no one could ever know there'd been a house in this clearing.

So when the officers asked me what I'd seen the day before, I lied and said I wasn't sure, that I hadn't been feeling well. And I tried to ignore my father when he sputtered and looked at me in reproachful surprise. I tried to think only of Maddie getting better.

It wasn't easy.

Would I have done things differently had I realized then that my parents' marriage wouldn't survive this final disappointment? That Mom would stay angry and Dad would have to move out, leaving Maddie and me behind?

I would not. Because miraculously, Maddie did get better. Better and better until the doctors said she'd completely outgrown her lung problems. Only I knew the truth, or thought I did.

Dad and I didn't talk much after that, so it was Maddie who told me when he gave up trying to sell the Eighty, and its timber. It seemed no one wanted to do business with a man who believed in magic houses.

And now he'd left it to me. I wondered why—if he could have possibly known, or guessed, about the bargain I'd made that day. Had we been a team all these years without me realizing it? Or had he left me the Eighty simply to remind me that I'd sold him out?

Perhaps it was that the fairies had whispered in his ear—just as sometimes, when I hold the key, they whisper in mine.

GENEVA: INTO THE WOODS
by Cara Reinard

The breeze through the open window pushes icy fingers down the buttons of my blouse, and I shiver. I can't believe I'm back here again. The same lace curtains tickle my face. They were white when I was a little girl and they're yellowed now from sunlight and time, but this place is still the same.

Beautiful and haunting.

Secrets buried so deep beneath the floorboards, I'm surprised it's still standing. But Judith, the owner, would never let it fall.

It's nearing quiet time at the inn—early November at Geneva on The Lake. I breathe in the fresh air, so different from the Manhattan dormitory smog, I can feel my insides compress and contract. It's only been a few weeks since I left school, but it's too early to think about why. If I start to think about *him* now, I won't be able to stop all day, so I focus on the water instead, the large expanse I'd skipped dreams across when I was just a girl.

They call them finger lakes.

Sometimes I imagine them as so—long appendages stretching as far as the sky. My mother would say today the lake's surface was pulled as tightly as a sheet, but that's only because she prided herself on how well she could make a bed. After tending to the inn for more than twenty years, who could blame her?

On the lake this morning there was a fresh coat of frost too thick to paddle through yet not nearly frozen enough to attempt a skate. The leaves have all turned their predictable shades of reds and yellows and oranges, and I'm already counting down the days until they've all turned brown and drifted from their branches. They usually fade and crumple to the ground like used paper bags in the wind between the Sunday after Thanksgiving and the last day of buck season—when the whole town goes dark.

No one will want the wine from the vineyards. It will be too cold for wine.

"Anabel, stop daydreaming and fix the linens. The Thackers will be here any minute." Judith speaks of the Thackers as if she's known them all her life, but she doesn't know any of the occupants here, because there are no regulars at the inn.

"I'm waiting for them to dry," I answer.

"They're not ready yet?" Judith is yelling at me, and I should be irked, but yelling is Judith's normal, and she's actually in a better mood when she has something to complain about.

"Well, as soon as they're done." She trots away.

I roll my eyes. Judith doesn't realize I've faced far uglier evils than her since I left here.

They still haven't found *him* yet. And as the weather changes and the snowflakes fall, all I can think about are his bones buried beneath the silky pines.

I take a deep breath and walk to the laundry room, but I can still hear Judith's heels click clack behind me.

"Where is Walt and why didn't he fix their room last night?"

"He said he had to go fishing," I yell from the laundry room.

"The lake's not even frozen yet. Old goat." Judith's voice is laced with resentment and it makes me wonder about marriage. Maybe if my own father hadn't deserted me in utero, I wouldn't have left the dead boy in the woods and run home.

"I'll have them ready before the guests arrive."

"It's all in the linens, Anabel."

I roll my eyes as she walks away. It's Judith's favorite saying, *"It's all in the…"* She'd fill in the blank with whatever worked that day—pies, hand soap, lotion, tea. I understood what she meant—that it was all in the little details, but I wish she could just say that.

The dryer buzzes.

"Anabel!" She's right in my face. Her gray-blue eyes storm beneath her modest lashes. She had to keep up her humble innkeeper's look. When I came back from Manhattan she politely asked me to wipe the smut off my face and to get into character.

"The Amish are a ways more down Route 14," Walt had heckled her.

This is why I love Walt. Later, he and I went through all the different characters I was supposed to be playing.

Anne of Green Gables.

Laura Ingalls Wilder.

Maria von Trapp.

I could've passed for any one of them in the long-sleeved white shirt, puffed at the shoulders, complete with gaudy apron that Judith made us wear.

"Snap to it," she says. "I don't know what it is that's so impressive out that window. Just some frozen water and a bunch of dead trees."

And a dead boy. Beneath a tree. In the woods.

I shudder, open the dryer and pull out the sheets. They're toasty on my hands, and I think of how cold Will's body must be by now.

There goes the doorbell. *Shit.* The Thatchers are early.

I run to the foyer with the laundry basket in my hands and bump into Judith.

A cold sweat has started on her upper lip, filling in her laugh lines with slick anger.

I run up the stairs to fix the room without saying another word.

I hear Judith's shoes click up the stairs.

"Is it ready? Why isn't Walt back yet?" she asks, exasperated. Walt's job at the inn is the porter and the woodchopper, and the all-around general handyman.

"I don't know," I say, even though I saw him leave with his tackle box this morning. Judith used to have Walt by the testicles, but according to my mother, he began to ignore her a few years ago. Mother said it was either a direct result of years of abuse or Judith's embarrassing display of admiration for Bill Eisner, the local vineyard owner who delivers bottles of wine to the inn.

"Well, you're going to have to fill in for him." Judith nods at the luggage at the bottom of the spiral staircase and huffs away.

The only thing she and Walt have is this inn. I'm not sure if she wasn't able to have children, if they hadn't wanted any, or if the good Lord had just been wise enough not to bless her with any, but one thing is for certain—this inn is Judith's baby, and anyone who disagrees with how she runs it—beware.

After the Thatchers are settled, I retreat to my quarters, the small room I used to call home. I promised myself I wouldn't end up at this one-and-done bed and breakfast Upstate like my mother, but after what happened with Will I feel like I can't go back.

Will and I met only a couple of months ago, the third week of sophomore year. After he died, I told the administration I had to take an emergency leave of absence, family crisis. No one asked any questions. Not the school or my mother or even the police. Will wasn't the kind of kid anyone went looking for.

I can't say I was in love with him, but I was in love with his energy. His spirit. He found me at a campus party, but he didn't go to school there. When I try, I can't even remember who he was with at the party. So sheltered from growing up in this town, my desire for adventure hadn't waned a day since I'd dropped my bags in the freshman dorm. Will fed that desire with his wild eyes, his quest to surprise me, concerts in the park, art exhibits in the city, drinks at posh places I didn't know existed.

After that first party, he was in my room every night with new things for us to try, and I was a junkie for his love of all things new.

Croton State Park.

He said we needed to go there, get out of the city, only a fifty-minute ride on the train. There's a lake there, he said. We will be freer there, he promised.

Lakes will always remind me of entrapment now.

When we arrived, Will said he had a surprise for me, but I needed to hike for the full experience. It was darker by the time we reached the spot. And colder. I could see my breath in the night air when he pulled the pills from his pocket. I wasn't a drugger, but I didn't say no, because this was one more experience I needed to have with Will, no different than the others.

My life had been one pulled sheet after another, and I needed to live.

So, I swallowed the pills with him.

He took more than I did, I don't know how many.

I shut my eyes for a moment, and when I opened them the stars all shot across the sky, the night turned to day, the flowers grew. Will was a prince and a knight, a monster and an angel, and when I woke up, minutes or hours later, he was none of those things.

He was just dead.

Foam had frozen on his face, and I was so cold, I couldn't feel my fingers.

But I made myself bury him anyway with leaves and pine needles. I took as many thick needles as I could and spread them all over his body, convinced they would make a better blanket than the leaves, keep him warm. I cried so hard, the tears splashed his face. It was frozen open in an expression I cannot forget. It steals my sleep, my life sentence for being an adventurous twenty-year-old.

I did not love this boy.

No one would miss him.

But, they might hold me responsible for leaving him there, an accessory. Besides, I was taught to cover up this sort of thing. As long as we didn't talk about it, it didn't exist. So, I ran home to the place where I learned to keep these kinds of secrets.

My mother taught me best.

Today is her day off, and I'd resisted pulling out the map every day I'd been here for fear she'd find it. But I finally had a moment alone. The old wooden dresser makes a scraping sound as I pull it out and remove the map buried underneath a pile of old sweaters. It's not a map, really, more a pamphlet I picked up on the train now dotted with mile markers on the road to the spot where I exited the woods—where I left Will. I scribbled down some trees too, a number of footsteps, the direction—east of the road. It looks like a preschooler's map, but I could find his body again if I tried.

But, I knew I never would.

The drugs hadn't been my idea, they were Will's.

I lay in bed and stare at the map, the inked characters, a smudge of something pink, and a fingerprint. I wonder if it's part of Will. I fall asleep with him on my chest.

When I awake in the night, there is screaming. I'm not sure if it's my own or not, because I'd been waking up screaming a lot.

But then I hear her, screeching like an owl. I peek my head out of the window and there Judith is, with Walt, beating his chest with her fists. Walt has his tackle box with him in the dead of the night. He drops the box, and holds her fists so she stops hitting him.

The tackle box is half open and the contents spill all over the patio.

There is no bait, no tackle, no fishing equipment at all. Instead, there are clothes shoved inside, and a ring of keys that have fallen out.

"Who is she?" Judith asks in her pained voice. I shut the window, because I know how this story ends.

Walt, you dog. He had gone *fishing.*

I go back to bed, but sometime in the middle of the night, I hear the wood chipper running in the backyard. When Walt really needs to get away from Judith, he saws branches that don't need to be hacked. Purees them so fine, he turns them into a gerbil's playground.

The next day, the Thatchers leave early and Judith doesn't come out of her room. My mother comes in shortly after eight to prepare the breakfast biscuits. I fill her in on the happenings on the patio.

"Oh my!" Her gentle eyes are abashed. "Well, you know how it works here. We have to pick up the slack."

My mother feels an odd servitude to Judith for taking her in when she was an unwed mother. And for helping her get rid of the second pregnancy, the one we don't speak of. The father had been a married tenant who'd shown a liking to my mother. My mother was lucky, Judith had always said, that she had Judith's resources— the butcher's station she set up in the basement to rid the other pregnancy so Judith's inn wouldn't be exposed as a brothel.

I swear the smell of ether is still embedded in the basement floor. I haven't been down there a day since I turned ten, and I still can't go, the loss of the sibling I never knew stronger than the old nails holding the house together.

Maybe that's why I left the dead boy beneath the tree in the woods and ran home.

Judith stumbles from her room, hair in a knot, fully clothed.

"Hello Darcy, hello Anabel," she says, business as usual. "Ah, the biscuits, good, the Fiores will be here any minute. It's all in the biscuits, you know?"

"Absolutely," my mother says.

The Fiores's arrival goes off without a hitch, and shortly after they arrive, old Bill Eisner pulls up with a fresh crate of wine.

"This is nearly double your regular order of red. Having a party?" he asks.

"Of sorts. Feel free to drop by later if you'd like to celebrate."

Bill chuckles, but he neither declines nor accepts her invitation.

Walt doesn't return that evening, but it's odd that the wood chipper starts around the same time as the night before. I have enough of my own problems falling asleep to pass judgment on how Judith spends her evenings. But, I do begin to wonder when Walt still doesn't return the following day. The house is especially quiet without him.

The last night the Fiores are in town, two other couples arrive, and Judith does something she's never done before. She invites over some of the other townspeople for an open party. My mother and I work overtime on appetizers and special dishes, and we aren't sure why Judith is giving away all of this free food. She cracks open the wine from Mr. Eisner, who has decided to show up after all. She also insists on fixing everyone's drink in her fine crystal goblets and the party is actually fun, the wine very good.

"I've drunk my own wine before, of course, but it tastes especially fine out of these beautiful goblets," Bill says.

"It's all in the crystal, Bill." She winks at him, and it makes him blush.

Even my mother can't help but giggle.

The news spreads quickly of Judith's fine wine, and soon she is selling Bill's wine out of the inn, but she has insisted on uncorking it first and giving away one of her signature corkers with the Inn's name plastered on the side, free advertising.

A few days after the party, the police arrive. They say a woman went missing, a librarian who lives in Ithaca, said to be associated with Walt. The librarian's colleagues say they saw Walt nosing around town with her.

"I don't know where my husband is. He told me he was leaving me a few nights ago and I haven't seen him since."

"Do you know if he was leaving you for this woman?" They hold up a photo of a pretty blonde lady.

"I have no idea, but I wouldn't doubt it."

"Do you mind if we take a look around?"

"Take all the time you need," she says, cheerfully. "Here, take a bottle of wine with you too. Big seller."

The cops take one bottle each. "Here's a sample." She hands it to the older cop.

"I shouldn't drink on the job."

"It's just a thimble." Judith chortles.

He takes a little swig. "Wow, that is good. A little bit of a woodsy taste, isn't there?"

My stomach drops to its bottom, and my mother stops cutting the pears for the pear pie. The officers leave the inn without finding a clue.

"Where's Walt, Judith?" I ask.

"Well, I don't know," she says.

"Did you do something to Walt, Judith?" I ask.

"Ana," my mother whisper-screams. "It's none of your business."

"Dear, we take care of each other here, remember? Don't ask me where Walt is and I won't ask why you wake up screaming in the middle of the night, or where that map leads that you keep hidden in the basin of my dresser."

I almost slice off my finger, I'm so taken aback.

"Oh Anabel," she laughs. "I know every square inch of this place. It speaks to me when new things come in and go out."

And, I'm stuck, just like when she killed my sibling. I couldn't tell anyone back then because my mother would lose her job and I can't tell anyone about Walt because she'll tell them where Will is. But still, she couldn't have done what I think she did.

"But Judith, *where* is Walt?"

My mother doesn't stop me from speaking this time because I know she wants to know the answer too.

Judith lets out another laugh, deep and sinister. "Oh Anabel, it's all in the wine, my dear. It's all in the wine."

TRAIN WRECK
by Kathleen Shoop

Ellie Trumbull squinted out the window of the Uber, gripping the door handle. The car swerved and bounced up the long driveway leading to the retreat center where the courts had sent Ellie for punishment. She grabbed her stomach to stave off nausea, but when it began to launch itself she smacked the driver's arm. He slowed and stopped. Ellie pulled the handle, and tumbled out of the door onto all fours, heaving.

She gasped for breath, dizzied. Voices sounded as she struggled to stand. She focused on the group heading toward her: two women, a man, and several children who simply bolted past her, their squealing laughter filling the air.

A graceful woman with gray, bunned hair and dark skin approached. She took Ellie's arm and pulled her close, leading her into a building. "Welcome. I'm Vera."

"I'm Alice." A stout woman with platinum spiked hair followed along.

A lanky man with hair so perfect it looked plastic picked up Ellie's duffel bag. "I'm Brandon. Your husband'll send the rest of your luggage shortly."

Ellie grunted. They led her upstairs. Brandon rushed ahead to open a door. Ellie shuffled inside.

"Your room," he said. "I'll set your bag here."

Ellie looked over her shoulder to see him smiling, as he'd been doing since she arrived. "Thanks, Guy Smiley."

"What?"

She ignored his question, held onto one of the top bunks and surveyed the space. Three large windows at the end of the room and three sets of bunks with plastic mattresses belted the perimeter.

Ellie collapsed onto a bed.

"Plastic makes it easy to clean," Vera said.

"Shut those." Ellie shook her hand at the windows.

The woman sighed, closed the curtains and lowered the blind that covered the center pane. She lifted Ellie's feet off the floor and swung them onto the bed. "Housekeeping'll make up the bed in a little bit."

"Fine," Ellie groaned.

Vera loosened Ellie's shoelaces.

Ellie snatched her feet away. "I'm *fine*."

Vera backed away, her large hands flailing for a moment before she tucked them against her belly. "Our healing circle begins in an hour."

Ellie turned away and balled up. *Leave me alone.*

And a few seconds later the door clicked shut.

***

Giggling children and the sound of feet running down the hallway outside Room 2 woke Ellie. Her mouth was desert dry, so she headed downstairs to the great room where she saw a kitchen area. With the kids gone, the silence felt good.

Ellie startled at the sight of Alice, Vera, and Guy Smiley sitting around an island. Guy Smiley poured coffee. Healing circle.

"Ellie," he said. "Welcome."

Vera sliced banana bread. The scent threatened Ellie's stoic facade. A smile tugged her lips, but she tucked away the fleeting happy sensation, hid it where it wouldn't remind her how Maggie's face would light up when she bit into her favorite treat.

Alice clomped her feet onto the coffee table. Vera batted them away and pushed the banana bread toward Ellie.

She looked away.

"I'll take hers," said Alice.

"I'd like to begin," Vera said, her voice gentle and melodic. "The healing circle guides us into continued acceptance and strengthens our endurance as we grow through the pain that comes with losing a child. Each of us understands the daily shock of waking and realizing our lives will never be the same. So how do we go on?"

Guy Smiley sipped coffee. "Feels good to be with everyone."

"Each time we meet I do better back home," Vera said.

"Same," Alice said.

"We hope you'll find our group helpful, Ellie," Vera said.

When Ellie didn't respond the others went around describing how they lost their child. Ellie blocked out every word, rubbing her temples. Her own pain was enough. She wasn't about to invite theirs inside. Her gaze strayed to the kids outside, the game of tag that left them breathless, rolling down the hill and out of sight. How lucky they were.

"Ellie?" Alice asked. Ellie turned her gaze back to see Alice glaring.

"It'll help," sweet Vera said. "To share."

Guy Smiley slid forward in his seat, fingers steepled. "Change brings...blah, blah ... comfort, healing..." He droned on and on and finally Ellie's mind snapped back to what he first said.

"*Change*?" Ellie said.

He nodded. They all did.

Ellie's anger surged. She wiped spittle from her lip. "I don't *want* change. I feel Maggie more now than I ever did... before she died I couldn't wait to get to work, or girls' night out or go away with my husband. My daughter... difficult from the day she was born... is dead. I'll *never* sit with you people thinking about change and eating stinking banana bread."

She stood and stomped away.

"She don't want help," Alice said.

"But her husband..." Brandon said.

Ellie got farther away, unable to hear what they said. Her husband? He was finished with her. She jogged to her room and crashed onto the mattress that housekeeping hadn't yet returned to make. She covered her face and held back tears. With balled fists she tried to resist.

But she couldn't.

Up off the bed, Ellie dug through her duffel and found it. Vodka. Cap unscrewed, she gulped, washing away the scent of banana bread, the thought that she'd never again see Maggie's smile when she took a bite of it.

***

Ellie slept in fits, waking and noting the ribbon of daylight that had outlined the window blind had blackened. Satisfied that none of her captors were going to fetch her for another healing circle, she fell back asleep, slumber being the portal to the only peace she found each day.

***

Something startled her. She rolled toward the center of the room and rubbed her eyes, mind fogged. What was she seeing? She squinted at whiteness that shouldn't be there. Slowly the gauzy haze took shape. Two girls wearing white dresses, holding flower bundles, smiled at her. The little one dropped her flowers and the older girl squatted to collect them. Ellie sprung from bed to help. As she neared, they disappeared. She brushed her hands over the rug. No flowers. Ellie exhaled, shutting her eyes and opening them again. Gone. She shook her head. The vodka had done its work.

***

The boozy dream wouldn't allow Ellie back to sleep so she dragged downstairs with her vodka. Coffee. She shambled to the machine, selected coffee, added a filter to the basket and dumped in the proper amount. With her tired eyes practically closed she filled the pot with water to add it to the machine and pressed start.

It didn't take long before she realized that something was wrong. Water poured everywhere. She smacked at all the buttons trying to avoid the scalding water then yanked open drawers looking for towels.

"What in the heck…" A voice came from the other side of the island. A man with gray hair and a baseball cap stood there in his jeans and sweatshirt.

Panicked, she mopped the flood. "I don't know what happened, I just…"

He stomped over. She backed away while he stopped the water. He grabbed another towel and growled as he cleaned her mess.

He pointed at the side of the refrigerator. "Directions. Right there."

She shook her head, hopelessness flooding in like the hot water, shocking her at how fast the feeling could return.

He sighed. "I'm sorry. I thought the pipes had burst or something and then you stood up and I just reacted. Badly."

She ran her hands through her hair, catching her fingers in the knotted mass.

He studied her. "You need coffee."

"I do."

He moved a stack of papers that had been in the way of the water and set them on the island. She separated them, shaking them out, noticing lists of items like watches, shoes, inkwells. She held up a wet newspaper, the front page featuring a train wreck.

"I'm so sorry."

He patted her shoulder.

"No booze, you know." He gestured at her vodka bottle.

Her eyes widened. "Really?"

He nodded and reset the coffee machine. "Watch. Water is piped in. Just press start."

She shook out one of his papers. "I'm so sorry. When I make a mess it's always a big one."

He smiled and leaned on the island. "Ellie? You're Ellie."

"Messy Ellie, that's me."

He pulled a pipe and tobacco from his pocket and headed toward the exit. "I'm Bill." He walked out and left her staring after him, the vodka still clutched in her hand.

***

After a pot of coffee, Alice, Vera and Brandon came for her. They frog-marched her up a mountainside, across a field and into another wooded path.

Vera pointed toward a gigantic red balloon suspended in air. "Pamper Jump. It's called that because people generally need Pampers after climbing it."

Ellie nodded and started to walk on.

Brandon grabbed her wrist. "We're doing this."

Alice plugged her hands on her hips. "I hate this thing."

"You said you'd go first," Brandon said.

Alice puffed out some air. "Strap me in."

They hooked her into a harness, attached and checked the connections. Ellie watched, disbelieving. Alice had to be sixty-five years old. The others were at least that old. Ellie looked around, feeling as though there must be cameras recording her response and that she was to stop the madness.

Vera and Brandon grabbed ropes and gathered in a clump.

"Come on, Ellie," Brandon said. "We need to break her fall."

Alice pointed at Ellie. "Don't trust her on my ropes."

Ellie cringed. She would just leave them to their demise if she didn't question whether any of them could pull themselves up a few inches let alone scale giant staples that created steps straight up a tree. One hundred feet.

Alice climbed like a spider monkey, her chunky body moving light and quick. She mumbled the whole way up, punctuating with groans and "This sucks."

She got to the top and the tree swayed back and forth. Ellie's throat dried. Alice wobbled, putting one foot on to the top of the flattened treetop then the other and she rose to standing, arms spread. Ellie couldn't breathe.

"All right, Alice," Brandon said.

Alice lifted her leg backward in an arabesque, causing everyone to inhale sharply. Then she swung her leg forward, flew into the air and smacked the giant red balloon with an angry fist. She went into a free fall, arms and legs splayed, wiggling.

It wasn't until Ellie felt hands pulling her up that she realized she'd dropped to the ground and balled up, screaming. The way Alice fell through the air transported Ellie back to Maggie getting hit by the car. Time had slowed as Maggie hung in the air just long enough for Ellie to believe she could catch her little body.

***

Ellie bolted. She barely stopped before plummeting over a hillside. Alice was on her heels. Ellie slid down the hillside grabbing onto vines and tree limbs that gave and held her as she descended. Alice screamed.

Finally making it to the bottom, she came to a frothy stream, a wire cable strung across it. Wires extended from the main cable and two others connected to make handrails. She stepped onto the cable and started across. Gazelle-like, she moved until her foot slipped. She lost her grip and tumbled into the rushing water. Her shoulder hit the bottom. Pain seared. She fought the urge to inhale underwater. *Just stay here, let everything go… No use fighting.* Even the booze didn't really do the job anymore.

A strong grip pulled her up from under the water and Ellie came face to face with Alice.

They heaved for breath.

Alice collapsed, water splashing past them. "Not gonna baby you," Alice said.

"You're a mean, awful person."

"I'm real."

"Real friggin' mean."

"Truth hurts," Alice said.

"Stupid saying."

Alice pointed her finger. "You're in trouble, little lady. You've a husband who still loves you for some Godforsaken reason. You staggered into traffic drunk, causing an accident. Do you care about anything except your own pain? You keep *that* tight and cozy, stuffed into your heart, locked up in that fourth chamber, right where you can reach it easy, same as you reach for that bottle. Looking at ya, I can't imagine which you like better, that writhing mass of pain in your chest or the booze."

Ellie looked away, icy stream water numbing her legs and hands.

Alice sighed. "Your sorrow don't give you permission to hurt others."

Ellie flinched. She'd been trying to forget about the accident she recently caused.

"You oughta be thanking the good Lord you didn't take someone's daughter from *them*."

Ellie stared at the water swirling around her body. "How in the hell do you know any of that?"

"Facebook."

"I'm not on Facebook."

"Oh, yes you are."

Alice stomped out of the stream "And take a brush to that hair, would ya? It's a nest a rat wouldn't even live in."

Ellie kept her lips sealed but couldn't keep from shooting Alice the finger.

Alice frowned, wiping mud from her knees before stalking away.

Down stream, children played, those summer voices, laughing, yelping, teasing.

As Alice left, the kids waded into the water. Ellie preferred not to see or hear them. She got up and trudged past a sign describing a train crash. It was the same wording she'd seen in the newspaper article she'd gotten wet that morning. She ought to make a sign for herself; a sandwich board to explain why no one should bother with her. "Train wreck." She thought of the accident Alice mentioned and doubled over. A seed of a different type of pain formed inside. She never meant to harm anyone else.

***

Ellie lay in the grass at the top of the hill near the lodge. The hot sun dried her clothing stiff and starched her hair with stream debris. Eventually, Vera fetched her for dinner. Ellie sat at the island, embarrassed.

Guy Smiley walked in. Blue sports coat, checked shirt and tie. He wiped the top of his leather shoe with a napkin then washed his hands. "Crepes. Peanut butter." He grinned and dug in.

"Remember that recipe last year when Luke Smutney was here?" Vera said.

"That eggplant tofu raisin thing?" Alice shuddered.

"He had a different sensibility," Vera said.

Ellie nibbled, realizing this was one of her favorite meals. They'd been talking to her husband. "That's how this works? You make favorite recipes for the latest drunk you want to heal?"

They stared at her.

"You think you're here because you're a drunk?" Guy Smiley said.

Ellie froze and considered it. "Well yes. The judge said."

Vera set her fork down and turned to Ellie. "He sent you here to heal your heartbreak, not to punish you for drinking."

"Punishment'll come with jail time," Alice said.

Ellie's eyes widened. Hearing those words aloud chilled her every time.

***

Ellie ate, silent, angry. Bill brought in her suitcase. "Just delivered," he said.

She dragged it upstairs and popped it open, rifling through it. "Please don't let Christopher have found my travel vodka, please." She felt deep inside the inner pocket, left hand side. There it was. She pulled it out and drank down the whole thing.

***

Pulling, tugging, pain. Ellie shot out of bed, hand to her head where someone had been yanking on her hair. She rolled up the shade, letting the moonlight in. A glint on the bedside table caught her eye. A brush: heavy, silver, a wild mass of flowers made the handle. Had her husband packed it and she didn't remember using it?

Alice.

Ellie stalked into the hall and rapped on Alice's door with the brush.

No answer.

She banged again.

The door swept open. Alice stood with a CPAP mask strapped to her face, eyes wide then narrowed with anger.

Ellie shook the brush. "You put this in my room."

Alice ripped off her mask. "That's not mine."

Ellie glanced at the brush then scowled. "Stay out of my room."

"Stay outta mine," Alice said.

***

Ellie woke before daylight wanting coffee.

Bill entered with his stack of papers.

She raised her mug. "Did it right this time."

He set papers down next to her. "Progress."

He flicked on the lights and sat beside her.

"Where'd you get that brush?"

She debated lying, afraid he'd think she stole it.

She shrugged. "In my room."

He flipped through his papers and pointed to a list. "Right there. Silver brush, wildflowers…"

"What's that?"

"Inventory. Historical society wants to showcase the Wilpen items and this one's been missing since we found a train case in 2006."

She shook her head. "Wilpen?" It sounded familiar.

"The 1912 train wreck."

They stared at the brush.

"Well, the historical society will be happy. Thank you, Ellie."

***

The day brought another healing circle and trip to the Pamper Jump in which Ellie witnessed Vera scaling it blindfolded due to it being too easy for her. Again, Ellie couldn't stomach watching them fall, couldn't try it herself. That night with no booze to soothe her, she took a bath.

In and out of sleep, she tossed, arm flung off the side of the bed.

She woke to someone brushing her hair. Startled at first, she considered opening her eyes. Something made her stop. She stayed in the dream, the sensation of her hair being brushed like she and Maggie used to do before sleeping. Precious nightly time shared and forgotten. Now Ellie felt the memory cushioned inside a dream.

Mischievous laughter and whispering pulled Ellie toward consciousness.

She opened her eyes to see the girls in white again. But this time they had a third by the hand: small, with dark curls spiraling down her back.

Maggie.

She put her lips to Ellie's ear. "I'll stay with you, Mama."

Ellie bowed her head, tears burning. Maggie wrapped her thin arms around her mother, patting her back. Ellie stayed suspended in the dream, cradled by the connection to her daughter.

"Then you'll come for me," Maggie said. "Someday."

The sensation shook Ellie. She shuddered and began to cry. Finally, she let the pain course through her.

***

Ellie put away the clean dishes while drinking coffee. Bill came in with a box. He dug inside and pulled out the brush Ellie had found.

"It belonged to the Rhody girls. Six and twelve years old."

Ellie thought of the girls who brought Maggie, giving Ellie the first sliver of comfort she'd felt in two years. *I'll stay with you, Mama.*

She drew a deep breath. They'd been trying to get her attention since she arrived. Would she even be able to explain this to Christopher? He'd put her away.

"Can't believe you found it," Bill said.

***

Two days later Ellie sat having coffee as the sun rose over the treetops in the distance. Voices drew her attention and she turned. Guy Smiley wore pajama pants, his helmet hair looking like corn stalk tops. Vera's bun was out and her kinked hair stood on end like tufts of cotton. Alice gestured at her head. "This is as messy as mine gets." The spikes were as usual, stiff, foreboding.

"Why aren't you combing your hair? Brandon. You're a disaster." A laugh bubbled up inside Ellie.

"You think we don't feel the same pain you do," he said. "It's not that. We've just learned to brush our hair and wash our clothes and awaken inside the pain each day. We've made callouses on our hearts."

"We want you to see our insides the way we see yours," Vera said.

"It never stops," Alice said.

"There's a junkyard in that clearing across the valley." Vera pointed. "You can barely see it because it's surrounded by so much beauty."

"We all have hidden ugly parts," Brandon said. "But the ugly isn't all of us. We look past that junkyard nearly every time we gaze over the valley to see the beauty."

"I want to leave," Ellie said.

"We know," Alice said.

"No matter where you go, the loss, that junkyard'll go with you," Vera said.

Alice touched her arm. "Broke it once." She tapped her thigh. "Broke this too. Same accident. Leg hurt so bad, couldn't feel the broken arm."

Ellie shook her head.

"You're breaking your own leg to cover up the pain in your arm," Alice said.

"You're allowed to feel the loss. Don't cover it up," Vera said.

She nodded.

"Can I call my husband?"

Brandon handed her his phone and they all left.

"Hello?"

"Christopher?"

"Ell?" he said through a sigh.

She couldn't speak, tears choked her voice.

"I'm here," he said.

She sobbed.

"I don't know where to start," she said.

"Ell." He drew and let out a deep breath. "We're in the middle. You don't have to start."

"We're?"

The line was silent.

"Do you want me to come?" he asked.

"You would?"

More silence.

"Yeah. Yeah. I would."

A MINDFUL CHANGE
by Martha Swiss

Takumi Nakano practically sprinted up the forest trail. His breath came out in little puffs in the chilly mountain air. He felt invigorated, alive, and thrilled to be taking a meditation walk at his first Mindful Writers Retreat. And it was working! Already, ideas for several stories formed in his mind. He was too excited to stop and jot them down in the little notebook he'd received when he arrived. He didn't want to stop climbing the steep hill behind the conference center lodge for fear the ideas would stop. He felt drunk on this newfound wellspring of creativity.

But his reverie snapped when he nearly tripped over a fallen tree. Annoyed, he looked around the forest then at the deep layer of decaying leaves at his feet. He was a little startled to realize he had strayed off the trail, which was nowhere in sight. No problem. He'd always had a good sense of direction and would allow his instincts to lead him to a meadow that lay just east of here—he had seen the edge of it on his way up.

Takumi traversed the hillside, stepping over logs and ducking under branches, and quickly found the meadow. Just where he knew it would be. All he had to do was follow the edge of it and he'd end up above the lodge. His stomach growled and he realized it was probably time to go back for breakfast anyway.

Story lines and characters again bloomed in his mind. He soon reached the point where he felt the lodge should be and looked down the hill, but all he saw were meadow and forest. Nothing looked familiar. Mildly annoyed with himself, he decided to take a different tack: go to the top of the hill and look down. Surely he'd see the main road and the long driveway snaking up to the lodge, as well as the rooftops of the conference center through the leafless trees.

It took longer to hike to the top than he'd thought, and he arrived out of breath. Without pausing, he strode across the meadow, an expansive space that seemed at the top of the world. He came to what he thought would be the spot located directly above the lodge and looked down. He only saw trees below—no road, driveway, or rooftops. He looked to the horizon where a tower with a red blinking light stood. *That must be the tower we saw last night when we came outside to watch the thunderstorm*, he thought. He gazed west of the tower and saw a second tower with a red blinking light, identical to the other. Was *that* the one they had seen last night? At that point he realized he was completely disoriented and had no idea where he was, except on a hilltop in a meadow in the Laurel Highlands.

The first pangs of panic rose from his belly to his throat. He briefly wished for a rescue helicopter to drop out of the sky, but knew that was irrational. Pushing down his fears, he turned and began pacing across the meadow in the other direction, not sure of his plans but thinking it would be best to keep moving. He got halfway across the meadow and a cold drizzle began to fall.

Takumi flipped up his hood and did a quick assessment of his situation, panic again clawing at his throat. He rationally ticked through several positives: he was well dressed for the conditions in a rain jacket and sturdy boots. He wore layers of clothing and felt dry and warm. Even though he was seventy years old, the retired dentist was fit and in good shape. But he was hungry and realized he had no food or water. He hadn't eaten since dinner last night and no one knew where he was. Suddenly he felt tired and realized he should conserve his energy and use his head. He needed to think.

Takumi closed his eyes and took a few deep breaths to calm himself. He opened his eyes and slowly turned in a circle, scanning the meadow for clues on what to do next. He made a second turn and a third. On his third turn, he noticed a low grass hut that had escaped his notice before, perhaps because its tawny color blended with the tan vegetation of the meadow. He decided to check it out. If nothing else, it was shelter, and he could rest there until the drizzle stopped.

When Takumi was within a few yards of the hut, a short hunched man with wiry white hair suddenly appeared next to it.

"H-hello," said Takumi, startled.

"Hello," said the man. "Who are you?"

"I'm Takumi Nakano," said Takumi. "Who are you?"

"I'm Ivan the troll."

Takumi looked hard at the stranger and realized he really did look like a troll, even though he'd never seen one in person. Besides his wild shock of white hair, the troll had big hands and feet, stumpy legs and arms, and a round belly under his brown buckskin tunic and pants. His eyes were squinty, his teeth bad, and he had several warts on his face. Takumi always noticed teeth. He tried not to stare, but was shocked at the appearance of the troll. To break the awkward silence, he asked, "Where did you come from?"

"I live here," said the troll, matter-of-factly. "What brings you here?"

"I'm lost," said Takumi. "Maybe you can direct me back to the conference center?"

"Can't get there from here," said Ivan, absently picking his teeth.

"What do you mean?" asked Takumi, incredulous. "I just came from down there somewhere." He gestured vaguely with one hand.

"Nah, not that simple, friend."

"What do you mean?" asked Takumi.

"You came here for something," said the troll, leveling his gaze at Takumi.

"What? Stop playing games," said Takumi, losing patience. "I'm lost. I've been wandering around up here for an hour. I'm hungry and I don't have any water. Aren't you going to help me?"

"You'll be okay. Trust me," said the troll. "All you need to do is ask for a change. It's what you came here for."

"Change? Change of what? Clothes? Underwear?" asked Takumi, waving his hands.

"Just something you'd like to change in your life," said the troll, cracking his knuckles.

Takumi laughed. "Oh I get it, you're a genie who grants three wishes, right?"

"Not quite, pal," said Ivan. "I make changes. Everybody and their brother grants wishes. I'm in a different line of work. Besides, I don't like the whole lamp and bottle thing. I like my hut." He nodded in the hut's direction, then put his hands in his pockets and rocked back on his heels. "I serve a different market. Changes. And you get just one." He pointed a stumpy finger at Takumi. "None of this three business."

Takumi stared at the troll, wondering if he might have fallen in the forest and hit his head and this was all a dream. He looked up at the gray sky and felt the cold drizzle on his face. His stomach growled. No, he was very much in the here and now.

"If I ask for a change, will I get to go back to the lodge?" asked Takumi.

"Oh yeah," said the troll. "You're only here because you're seeking some sort of change in your life. You obviously had no idea you wanted a change. Anyway, once you ask me for the change, you'll go back to your normal zone. Take your time, I don't have to be anywhere today." The troll leaned against the hut, examining his fingernails.

Takumi paused and thought. He didn't know what all that meant, or how he would get back to the lodge. But what did he have to lose? He reflected on his life. He was more blessed than most. A wonderful wife, good kids, adorable grandkids, a wide circle of friends. He felt much younger than his age, the only clue of which was his salt-and-pepper hair. He had recently sold his successful dental practice and retired after forty years. He had looked forward to retirement and the chance to do lots of things he never had time for. Especially writing.

Takumi had written articles for dental journals throughout his career. What he really wanted to write was fiction, specifically action thrillers. But he didn't have a clue how to begin, so shortly after retiring he joined the Mindful Writers. Once a week he met with other writers at a library where they meditated then spent four hours writing. But it was hard, much harder than he thought it would be. He'd write a few sentences then spend the next hour revising them. The next time he read them he found them embarrassing and deleted them. He went round and round, getting nowhere. He thought maybe the retreat would spur his creativity and focus, and quiet his inner editor.

"I want to change what I write," blurted Takumi. "That's it, I want to write fiction now."

"That's it?" asked the troll, mildly surprised.

"Yes," said Takumi.

"No change to your bank account? Fancier car? No, uh, change in your love life?"

"That's it," said Takumi with a defiant lift of his chin.

"Okay, pal, whatever," said the troll, rolling his eyes.

In a flash, the troll leapt away from the hut and landed a few feet in front of Takumi. He waved his hands in Takumi's face and bellowed, "HOCUS POCUS YOU'VE GOT FOCUS! HERE'S SOME CONVICTION TO WRITE THAT FICTION!"

Takumi heard a loud bang and got swept off his feet. He spun in the air through a billowing cloud of light blue smoke that smelled faintly of strawberries. Soon the spinning slowed and the smoke lifted. He landed softly on his feet just outside the back dining hall door of the conference center. *What? How did I get here?* Takumi thought. He looked at his watch, 8:23 a.m. A little late to breakfast. *Wasn't I just in the woods?* He felt slightly perplexed, a little rumpled, and very hungry.

He looked around, then smoothed his hair, tugged his raincoat down, and yanked open the door. He walked down the hall to the dining room where his friends greeted him warmly. They made space for him at one of the tables, and the cook brought him pumpkin pancakes and bacon. He had never tasted anything so delicious and devoured every crumb.

After breakfast, he settled into his favorite chair by the fireplace. He turned on his laptop, fished his lucky writing crystal from his pocket, and began writing: "Once upon a time there was a troll ... ."

A HIKE THROUGH THE WOODS
by Madhu Bazaz Wangu

I fondly remember one of our hikes last year. The early spring air was fresh as we walked beside ancient banyan trees that had been planting the aerial roots into the ground through centuries. The trees stood guard over the low hills. The foliage above was at places so dense that it covered the sky. Further down, emerald ashoka and golden amaltas trees seemed to be vying in their beauty. Some of the trees were entwined with purple morning glory or pink clematis and some others with wild trumpet vine and butterfly pea. As the sun rose higher, parrots and pigeons flew down to the ground to peck at insects and seeds.

On our narrow pathway, at a clearing a peacock appeared from nowhere to show off its iridescent plumage, enlivening the small space. The thought of returning to that place and spending another day in those surroundings sent a wave of delight through me.

"We'll go on a different hike today," my husband announced. "You'll love it!"

Every year he would discover at least one new place for us to hike. Away from the hustle and bustle of the city in a forest through which ran a tributary of the River Ganges. Both of us found the new hiking places rather adventurous.

"Great!" I said excitedly. After two long monsoon months we were going to take full advantage of the sunny day.

We parked our 1963 VW Beetle and stepped out of the open parking lot to a small manicured entrance that ended at the edge of the forest. I inhaled deeply as we walked leisurely under the scented canopy of intertwining yellow and magenta bougainvillea. A passage of some hundred feet ended abruptly, leading to a pebbly path that trailed toward the slopes of the low hills. From the foothills, blossoming pink primrose, yellow button weed and white daisy bushes came into view. As we ascended, green ferns rubbed our ankles. The climb to the top was easy. From above, we could see a stunning scene of a river gorge below. The scenery took my breath away. I glanced at my husband. He was smiling contentedly, equipped with an umbrella that he insisted upon carrying. I held a water bottle.

We were in a good mood. We chatted about this and that until we reached a clearing that branched into two pathways. The marker was broken off its stake. But the trees marked with yellow squares were there to guide us. Were we to take a left or right turn? I asked. It didn't matter, we could go either way, he said. Though the path branched into several smaller treks it was more or less circular. If we stayed on track, it would end at the same place from where we started, he said, sounding certain.

We continued on the unpaved rocky path, chatting for a while, becoming quieter with each step until we were each lost in our own thoughts. Brisk walking had given rise to the warmth that swaths you when you sweat. I took several gulps of water and handed over the bottle to him.

We must have walked two or more miles when we heard distant thunder. Clouds had overcome the sun and the sky was getting darker. It began to drizzle. I was glad my husband insisted on carrying the umbrella.

Suddenly, we found ourselves in the middle of a storm. We sprinted down the path. But when wind joined the torrents of rain it seemed they were bent on beating us. Should we wait? Go back? We debated. It might get worse before it gets better. Let's wait for it to pass. We stood patiently under the umbrella.

My husband looked up at the trees.

"Weren't we following the yellow squares?"

I noticed a red circle on the trunk he was looking at.

"We didn't make a turn," I said.

"We must have!" He sounded annoyed.

"You said we were on a circular path. How could we take a wrong turn? 'Enter from one end and exit from the other' you said."

"I'm not the boss here. Why didn't you notice it when we took the wrong turn?"

"But you are the boss—with your sense of direction."

He did not respond. I was sure we would spot a tree with a yellow square. We had gotten lost before but then the weather conditions were not like this.

We decided to retrace our steps. The downpour got heavier. We stood still under the umbrella, close together, his hand on my shoulder.

The wind got brisk and changed directions. It started to blow so hard that the umbrella turned over and slipped from my husband's grip. We watched it fly away toward the sky until it vanished.

The downpour washed my husband's hair. His face looked pale and his eyelashes dripped. My black mascara, he said, was running down my chin and my black hair was soggy like a wet bird. I ignored him as I noticed the bright orange of my cotton shirt smearing my arms and white jeans.

Water bodies formed around us. Gushing forcefully, rivulets had joined together to create unrestrained streams. They were carving grooves in the mud, flattening the ground foliage and exposing pebbles.

It was the kind of rainstorm that drowned the memories of all the storms that we had ever experienced. We waited and waited for it to calm down. After what seemed like ages, the wind slowed down a little, but the torrents had no intention of stopping.

The storm seemed to bleach the landscape; the scenery had turned into a blurry black-and-white photograph.

After half a mile or so, to our combined relief, my husband spotted a tree painted with a yellow square. Our pace quickened. We must not have walked even a mile when we found our path blocked by a landslide. He looked at my frustrated face but didn't say anything. We turned back and took a different path, hoping it would take us to our car.

"Look!" he said, pointing to two fallen crisscrossing trees. "Didn't we see this on our way here?"

"Yes, we did! How much farther?" I asked, looking at my pruning fingers.

"I don't know. One, ten, a million miles?" he said.

"Why don't you know?"

"Why do you always expect me to know?"

A shiver shook my body. "Why is it raining so much? When will it stop?"

"Be patient! I remember seeing a couple of shelters on the map. I'm sure there is one somewhere here." He looked around. There was none. "If you imagine hard you might be able to conjure up one," he joked.

"Are you saying this to make me laugh? If you are, it isn't working."

"What else do you want me to do? I don't like it either. I'm trying to lighten the mood. Why should I be the one to cheer us up?" he cried in exasperation.

I didn't like myself for being sullen and irritable. I had turned his jolly mood sour. But my limbs were cold, and I felt tired. It had been three hours since we were lost. Our usual trekking time was never more than that. Too fatigued to continue, I slumped against the trunk of a fig tree. He slumped next to me. The ground was muddy. The earth seemed to be melting. I felt water rushing through the channels underneath my bottom.

The dripping rain mixed with the chilled wind went on and on and on. In a shallow grove about ten feet away, I noticed a dead peacock upside down. A shiver ran through my spine. I turned my head away. Thick fog appeared and made it seem colder.

I thought of a warm shower, dry clothes, cozy quilt and a book. I was tired of the pouring and banging and slamming of rain. The raindrops were stippling the muddy water, our heads and shoulders.

"This tree is of no help! The raindrops are beating on my head. I feel sore," I said.

"As they are on mine. Of all the days, I forgot to wear my hat today."

"I wish I was wearing one, too." My thick head of hair was of no use under the hard rain. "Oh, how long will this torture last?"

"This weather is certainly weird," he said, turning to me. "Imagine yourself walking under the summer sun. Okay?"

"What!"

"Imagination, use it! Imagine a glittering golden fireball in a cloudless blue sky."

"Okay." I humored him.

"Close your eyes! Feel dry clothes on your skin. We are listening to our favorite music, drinking hot tea and eating *garam* cheese *pakoras*."

"I tried."

"Try it again!"

I did not respond.

"You will forget all this once you are home under the warmth of a quilt. You can lay there as long as you want. I'll make dinner tonight."

I spotted another dead bird, this time a pigeon. What was next?

We got up and continued to walk.

"Of all the days, today I forgot to bring my compass. I am getting tired of all this," he said.

"Try to keep calm. Imagine summer landscape, dry surroundings the way you asked me to do." I tried to be kind.

"Look at me! Water is coming from each pore of my body. The tips of my fingers have begun to freeze." His palms had turned wrinkly and white, his fingers a tinge of blue. This worried me.

"Look at those blue bolts of lightning!" I said.

"Where? Where?" Before he raised his head, they were gone.

We walked over dozens of puddles.

"There it is!" he shouted and began to trot.

"There is what?" I fell in with his steps.

"Our car!" he shouted as he blinked, shielding his eyes with his hand from the rush of rain.

I could see a yellow blob at the edge of the parking lot. It had to be our VW.

"Looks like you are right. Thank God!" I said.

We smiled at each other.

"Finally! Come on!" he said.

"Let's stop at the first *chaiwalla* we see and order tall glasses of strong and sugary milk tea!" I said.

"Whatever you say, madam!" He chuckled.

We began to sprint. The blob grew bigger, its yellow brighter.

"Remember? When we got lost...in the hills of Mount Abu in Gujarat...under the heat of the summer sun, sweating like pigs...I hated the sun that day...the way I hate this rain."

We reached the car laughing. "Don't we have some almond chocolate left?" he asked as I rested my hand on the passenger side of the door handle.

"Yes, we do!" I smiled, water dripping from my parted lips. "Open the door quickly, please."

He put his key into the keyhole.

"What's the matter?"

"The key doesn't work! What the...!" he yelled.

The windowpanes were misted. I wiped the glass and looked in. My breath fogged it again.

He cleared the water dripping on the pane and looked harder. "This is not our car!" He said, "There are tennis rackets on the back seat!"

"Not the brown bag with almond chocolate? Our beach towels? The duffel bag with dry clothes?" I asked, almost crying.

It thundered again as the rain poured harder. The water ran down his balding head and on my washed eyelashes.

"Can't you somehow open this door? Can't we sit inside this car for a while?" I said.

"And go to jail?" He looked at me through the curtain of rain.

"So where is our car parked? Where is the *other* parking lot? How far do you think that is from here?" I cried, realizing it was his fault as much as it was mine. But instead I growled at him. "How far?"

"Let me think." He walked a few paces looking up the hill and toward the river. "Not far. Close by—maybe a mile away."

"Not far! Close by! A mile away!" I repeated his words in frustration.

"Don't scream at me! We could wait here for the owner of this car, get a ride."

"What if he is camping somewhere? He may show up...or he may not." I sighed, realizing the folly of his hope.

"We have to keep walking."

The raindrops got bigger and the rain got harder.

"I hate water!" I said.

"It won't take more than half an hour to reach the other lot." He consoled me.

"Half an hour for a mile?"

"In this weather, yes!" he emphasized with his usual confidence.

"What if our car went down the river and floated away because of a landslide? We were parked at the edge of the hill, remember?" I shuddered at the thought.

"Why such negativity? We'll have to get there to find out, won't we?" He began to lose his temper.

"I'm tired! I'm tired of this weather. I'm tired of these thundering clouds. This rain. I want to eat almond chocolate, drink hot tea with cheese *pakoras*."

He pulled me closer, kissed me on my watery lips, held my hand and began to jog.

"We'll be okay," he said.

I prayed.

We had been walking for four hours now. The sky was dark. It seemed as if the evening had set in.

"I've got to sit, take a break. Oh, God I wish we could sit under a banyan tree if the adventitious roots didn't hide creepy animals. I don't see any other tree big enough to protect us from these torrents. I could use a tree trunk to lean against and take a snooze." I moaned.

We did find a tree. Not exactly the kind I had imagined but close enough. Raindrops from the leaves pattered on our heads and shoulders. I covered my face with my hands. The rain hit my neck as I rested my head on my knees. Something crawled on my skin. A creepy touch. I leapt up and wiped my face, neck, arms and legs. I did not want to be touched. I stood up sneezing, coughing and choking. He stood up beside me.

"Let's make a move, it's getting dark!" he said.

"Just leave me here." I must have momentarily lost my mind because I said, "You go!"

"Please stop behaving like a child! I've no energy left to argue. It is not safe here. You know that—coyotes, foxes and who knows what else." He pulled me forward. "Let's go."

"I can no longer feel my fingertips."

He turned and rubbed my hands between his palms, one by one as I watched him.

"Okay?" he said. "Are you ready?"

I nodded. In our sneakers we plodded through the sludge.

"How long?" I asked.

"I guess fifteen more minutes."

"What? I can't hear you, speak louder!" I said, touching my ears.

"Can't you hear anything?" he said.

"What?" Rain had finally numbed me to the bone. "You go ahead. I don't think that parking lot is this way. And even if it is, our car won't be there. It is probably somewhere near where creeks and streams meet the river. I will just sit here under this tree." I stopped and was about to sit down. He held me by the shoulder.

"Get up and walk with me! You can't give up now after walking for more than four hours!"

"Just shoot me! And then go!"

"I would if I had a gun." He was who he was.

"Let me be."

"Stop this drama!"

"Drama! How much more dramatic can it get? You go! If you find the car, come and fetch me."

"It is getting dark. Remember that rope bridge? Let us walk up to that point then you can sit, and I will bring the car."

"I can't, I just can't, please have mercy!" I had nothing left in me.

But then I saw his point and dragged myself behind him. We floundered our way through streaming water and slushy puddles and strewn broken branches fallen on the path. I was fifty feet behind him. I managed to cross the rope bridge and stopped and leaned against its wooden post. Through the thinning veils of water and dim light of early evening a parking lot came into view. What if this was not our parking lot? My legs felt weaker than a minute ago.

"Is this the parking lot?" I shouted.

"Looks like it."

"Are you sure?"

"Yes, I'm sure!" he shouted and sprinted toward the lot. I saw him slip and fall. Quickly, he got up and then unconsciously wiped his hands on his muddy pants. He turned back to look at me, smiled sheepishly and stepped carefully.

There were streams of water rushing through the lot that did not exist when we arrived. My heart beat faster as a yellow VW came into view. My pace quickened as it became larger and familiar. I ran, ignoring the puddles as rain fell on my flailing arms.

My husband stood next to the door on the driver's side, too nervous to insert his key into the keyhole. I looked through the window and saw a brown bag lying on the back seat.

"Definitely ours!" I shouted.

He put in the key, turned it and twisted the door latch. He opened the door and before entering the car whooped triumphantly – the loudest I had ever heard from him. He sat for a moment, closed his door and beamed at me.

"Come in," he said.

"Unlock the car," I screamed from the other side.

"Oh, sorry." He unlocked the door.

The torrents had turned to a light shower. On the backseat were the brown bag of chocolates, towels, and the duffel bag.

With his palms over his eyes he exhaled, then pulled the towels from the back of the car and handed one to me. We dried our wet hair, faces and arms.

"Start the engine!" I said. The rain slowed down to a pitter-patter on the windowpanes.

"Off to the tea shop," he said, turning the key. The engine groaned. Then nothing.

"What was that!" I said. He tried again. This time there was a click and then nothing.

We are in the middle of nowhere, I thought and said, "Don't tell me you forgot to turn off the lights?" I shuddered.

He hit his forehead against the steering wheel several times and cursed in desperation that was not normal for him.

I NOURISH THE UNIVERSE AND THE UNIVERSE NOURISHES ME
by Madhu Bazaz Wangu

I watched as buoyancy pervaded my arms. My brown hair grew pale green leaves and bunches of mauve flowers. The chest hair grew into tendrils and the belly was bound in thin bark. My arms turned into branches; my legs into twisting trunk. My feet changed into roots penetrating the earth. Had I metamorphosed into wisteria? I did not know whether I was the tree or a man. I felt one with the tree. I had lost my ability to move but had gained some other sort of independence. Warm sun eased my shoulders and back; rain nourished my leaves and buds. I felt comforted, relieved of the stress I did not even realize I had.

Sweating profusely, I woke up in a desolate room. The dream felt so real that I touched my arms and head to see if I was myself or the wisteria. I was in a sanitarium, sent there at the tail end of my convalescence from a nervous breakdown. I was to live here until I regained my health.

Outside the building was bitter cold. I took a hot shower thinking of the project I had been working on just before I collapsed. For twenty years I had experienced deadlines, rat race, office politics, competition, backbiting, balancing budget, demotions, promotions, and then I was fired. The past bombarded my mind. I combed my hair and looked at myself in the mirror. Dark circles under my eyes and a pale complexion looked back at me.

A tray of breakfast was on the table facing the fifth-floor window. But I was not hungry for sanitarium food. I felt horribly lonely. I could not imagine my future. I threw myself face down on my pillow and burst into passionate sobbing. When the sobs stopped I found myself thinking of my teenage years. My parents died in a car accident when I was in tenth grade. I was an honors student. My grandmother looked after me. And then she passed away.

I felt like a disagreeable man with no future living a meaningless life. I looked out from the window. It had an expansive view of open space with vast forested area. Everything was covered with snow. From the main entrance of the sanitarium, a stone pathway led to the forest. In the middle of the dense trees a black circular wall seemed to enclose an empty space. The emptiness of the space tugged at my heart. I ground my teeth, cursing myself. I was angry and alone. I had never felt like this before.

A stream of awful and appalling thoughts continued to pass through my mind. How could they fire me? What if my health never recovers? Would I die and be forgotten? No one would know. No one would care. It was all very frightening.

My grandmother used to pray when she was afraid. The day she died I prayed. I had never prayed before, although she wanted me to. She wanted me to find God within.

I sat up and tried to pray. My thoughts shifted inward. I found myself in a dark shadowy place. I thought I might come across something, anything to comfort me, but when my eyes adjusted to the darkness, thoughts raced through my mind and obscured my view. I found myself with my memories and thoughts that I wanted to forget. The feeling I was left with was queer, quiet and gloomy. I tried to clear the cobwebs of my mind, but they stuck to my fingers and my arms: screaming, yelling, watching my back, hiring, firing. I descended into the gloomy darkness unable to penetrate my thoughts further or stay with my breath longer.

I turned and faced the breakfast tray placed on the side table by a caregiver. I was still not hungry. Twittering sounds were coming from the window. There was nothing else to do in the room. I wore my coat, gloves, boots and hat and walked down the stairs. I walked out through the main entrance of the building on the pathway leading to the woods and the wall. I walked past snow-covered trees, evergreens, climbers, bushes and flowerbeds.

The circular wall, made of black granite blocks, was eight feet high. The upper edge of the wall was covered with vines and creepers. The tops of the trees inside it were visible. To find an opening, I decided to walk around it. I walked for half an hour and realized I arrived at the same place from which I had started. The wall seemed to have no door. I heard a bird calling. I looked up, searching. On the largest branch of the tallest tree, I thought I saw a phoenix sitting with his magnificent iridescent plumage.

Since my childhood I had always wanted to see the beautifully breasted mythological bird, the phoenix, with its rainbow-colored train flowing majestically toward the earth. Its green, blue, red and gold plumage glittered under the sunshine. Sun rays blinded my view for a few moments. When my vision returned, the phoenix stood in front of me. Its magnificence brought a smile to my sour face. I stood gazing at the heavenly bird until it flew away. *Will I ever see the phoenix again? Where does he live?* I wondered.

I walked back to my room. Lunch was on the table. I knew I was supposed to eat but I was still not hungry. I lay down and closed my eyes. The image of a phoenix stayed in my mind's eye for a long time. In the dead silence the only thing I could hear was my breath going in and out. Thoughts about my work ebbed away. I had a glimpse of a maze of corridors. The one closest to me led to a hundred closed doors. Memories of my long-gone parents and the pain of their separation came rushing through. Tears rolled down my face.

"You must eat!" I heard the nurse say. "Otherwise, you won't get better."

"I know," I responded automatically. I looked away and wiped my eyes.

The next day, I walked back to the wall hoping to find an entrance and have another view of the fantastic phoenix. But I could find neither. I came back again and again. A walk around the wall became my daily routine.

One day, as I was walking close to the wall, something wonderful happened. A bird darted through the air. Was it him? It flew toward me and alighted on a big clod of earth. It was not a phoenix but a brilliant red cardinal. I watched him tilting his beautiful head to one side, looking at me curiously with his dewdrop eyes. We both sat there quietly.

"I'm lonely." I finally whispered to him, "May I call you Phoenix? Would you like to be my friend?"

He seemed to nod and stepped closer to where I sat. I wanted to pet him but was afraid he might fly away. We stood there looking at each other. Then he flew away.

When I returned to my room, I felt a bit hungry.

Next morning, I walked around the wall to visit my friend. I couldn't find him. I ran my second lap along the pathway. I fought against the cold wind that rushed at my face and held me back. Being outdoors stirred my blood. Big breaths of fresh air filled my lungs. I ran back to my room. I was sweating by the time I returned. I splashed my face with water in the bathroom and noticed a flush of red on my cheeks. My eyes looked brightened.

Weeks passed by. No longer did I glance disdainfully at breakfast or push away my lunch plate. I ate whatever I was served. I never missed my walk from the building and jog around the wall. But I missed seeing my friend Phoenix. Bare and long sprays of climbers that I now recognized as wisteria that covered the wall were swinging in the wind.

And then, one day as I was jogging, a gleam of iridescent red came into my view. I heard a welcoming sound. It was Phoenix coming toward me! When he stood close by me, I petted him on his soft feathery shining head. As I spoke to him, he seemed to understand, tilting his head left and right. Looking intently with his black jeweled eyes, he twittered and hopped between me and the wall.

"How are you?" he asked me.

"I'm fine. How are you?"

"It's so cold! Isn't it?"

"Yes, it is! Let's walk together and enjoy the warm sun and gentle breeze."

We walked together along the wall. "I missed you, Phoenix!" I said, smiling.

"Me, too."

After a while, he spread his wings and made a darting flight to the branch of a tree. The tree he perched on was inside the wall. How I wished I could enter the garden and see for myself what it was like.

"Walks seem to be helping you regain your strength and cheer you up," the nurse said, clearing my dinner plate.

I nodded. She was right. I felt physically stronger and mentally lighter, a bit awakened. I had begun to go outdoors every day. I didn't miss meals but was eating three meals a day. My nights were not fretful; I slept soundly. And I was no longer lonely; I had made a real friend. Good things were happening to me.

The following week rain poured down in torrents. The distant landscape remained hidden by gray mist and clouds. My friend, Phoenix, must be hiding in the lush foliage of the tree. There was no way I could go out.

I asked my nurse for a journal. She gave me a ruled notebook. I began to jot down my recent observations about being in nature, about Phoenix and about myself. I laid on my bed reading a book on gardening borrowed from the sanitarium library.

One day I dozed off and again wandered into a long corridor that branched into other corridors. All doors were shut. I walked up a flight of steps which led to yet more corridors. It seemed no one except I was in the huge rambling building. I walked for a long time without thinking of turning the handle of a door. One time, I tried to open a door, then another and the next. All were locked. Finally, I was able to open one with difficulty, only to face utter darkness. Everything was still. I was tired. I woke up. For several days the weather outside remained disagreeable. I was bored.

Then the rainstorm ended. The gray mist and clouds were swept away by the wind. The wind ceased. A brilliant deep blue sky revealed itself. I had never gazed at a sky so blue. Springtime was coming! I did not recall ever paying any attention to changing weather or getting excited about it. I wondered how it was in the innermost space where the Phoenix lived? Were there bulbs sprouting, green leaves and petals opening, evergreen bushes and wisteria climbers coming to life?

In the forested area one day, I heard a call and saw the Phoenix pecking the earth. He looked a bit shy, pretending he just happened to be there. Gladdened, I said, "You came to greet me, didn't you?"

I saw him smile and nod.

"You have changed my life, my friend! You have revived my spirit!"

He came closer.

I gently touched his feathery soft back. His red waistcoat was like satin. He puffed his breast out as if to show how proud he was. Then he hopped over a pile of freshly turned earth looking for seeds and insects.

"What is behind the wall?" I asked.

A gust of strong wind rushed down. Untrimmed branches of hanging ivy and wisteria waved, their trailing sprays swaying vigorously. I stepped closer to where the Phoenix had hopped. Behind the loose trails I glimpsed a doorknob.

My heart thumped. Phoenix tilted his head to one side as if he too was excited. My hand shook a little as I used both hands to turn the knob. The door creaked and opened slowly. I slipped through the door, let the cardinal walk in and shut it behind us.

We were inside the circle—the most magical and mysterious place I could imagine. The inside of the wall was covered with leafless stems of climbers so thick that they matted together. Numerous long tendrils looked like swaying curtains. I could not tell if they were dead or alive. There were flowerbeds and brown grass. There were evergreens and leafless bushes. And a small stream, its banks still covered with snow, meandered through the dormant garden. I breathed fast with excitement and wonder.

Everything was still; I could listen to the silence. Phoenix looked at me without stirring.

"Let's walk," I whispered. We stepped softly lest we awaken someone or something. Not even a sign of leaf or bud anywhere. Was this place dead? Beyond reviving?

I saw something sticking out of the black earth—a sharp tiny pale green point pushing through. I wondered what it was: crocus, hyacinth, or daffodil? I walked all over and carefully looked for other such sproutings. Hundreds came into focus. I searched and found a sharp piece of wood and a razor-edged rock. I knelt down and dug and winnowed out weeds until a little clear place was made around as many sprouting bulbs as I could manage. *Now they can breathe freely*, I said to myself.

An agile brown squirrel moved restlessly and inquisitively, a robin clinging at a branch flew down to watch me. A snow-white rabbit passed by sniffing with its quivering nose. As the earth was thawing, life seemed to emerge from nowhere.

Every day I spent hours weeding and clearing spaces around sprouting life. The top of the bulbs looked like onion tops. My gardening book said bulbs lived for years even if no one helped them. They helped themselves. They spread out underground and produced little bulbs.

I noticed brown lumps swelled on the thicker branches of the swaying tendrils. I touched them and felt more energetic and awake. The sun was nourishing vines and creepers, bushes and bare trees with its warmth and light as it was nourishing me. The rain was seeping through the space I had opened around the bulbs, reaching new growth. Phoenix, his plume getting redder with each day, kept me company.

At times the rain was heavy; at other times it just drizzled. When the rain was heavy I had to stay in my room reading or writing in my journal. I often found my thoughts drifting to a dark space. This time nothing obscured my view, no cobwebs of thoughts. I walked through a corridor and without any hesitation put my hand on one door handle. It turned without difficulty. This alarmed me. I waited for a few moments, took a long breath and pushed open the door. It opened to utter darkness. My thoughts had settled down. Slowly, a form emerged.

A few days later the sky was blue again. I jumped out of bed, ran to the window and opened it. The world looked touched by magic. All around life was struggling with all its might to sprout and grow through the black earth and brown grass was slowly turning green.

The sun was spreading gold. The circular space inside the wall started to look like a garden. Freshness pushed through everywhere. Flowers and buds that seemed dead until then were swelling. Purple and yellow crocuses were unfurling. The earth was waking up. Amidst this joy came a delight more charming than all—

my friend Phoenix was holding things in his beak to build a nest.

Who kept creating something out of nothing? Light from darkness? A cosmic dance from stillness?

Then one day, a new miracle was revealed. I saw six eggs in a cardinal's nest. A pale brown female cardinal was keeping them warm with her feathery breast and caressing wings. The wonder and magic outside made my inside stir. I felt it in my bones. In that rapturous realization, I threw up my arms exultantly and shouted, "I will revive! I will be healthy again! I will live!"

My old lifestyle had filled my soul with blackness. The air around me was poisoned with gloom. I felt disagreeable and dark. Now, new beautiful thoughts had pushed out the old hideous ones. A healthier life began to return to me. Blood began to flow freely, and strength flooded in. Sunlight nourished me and the earth; the wind swayed me and the tendrils. Bubbling water made me laugh and Phoenix, the cardinal, came down to the earth from heaven to be my friend. Quietly, something unbounded and released in me. I had forgiveness in my heart. Comforting thoughts guided me, and I was filled with gratitude.

A singular calmness had overcome me. *What is it?* I asked myself, passing my hand over my forehead.

"You are going to be discharged soon," my nurse said. "Your recovery in three months was magical. We were expecting you to stay for six."

"Nothing magical!" I said. "I nourished the universe and the universe nourished me." The words flew from my mouth. "But thank you! I do feel so much better."

The spring and summer months sped by. I was discharged from the sanitarium. The day I left, the outdoors was a wilderness of autumn gold and purple and violet blue and flaming scarlet and on every side were sheaves of white and ruby lilies standing tall. And in the foreground was the fabulous cardinal. He was accompanied by his female partner and their brood of six. Had they come to bid me farewell? The little chicks, with their chests held up high with pride, chirped.

I felt part of the cardinal's family. He had saved my life.

POETRY

THE GIRL IN ROOM 9
by Lorraine Bonzelet

Luggage hauling
Gifts enthralling
Windows flaunting fresh snow
Floorboards moaning
Gently groaning
On writers writing below

Friendly greeting
Humble meeting
New names, twelve in a row
Shanti vowing
Silent bowing
The writers writing in flow

Flames engaging
Fire raging
Vibrant orange and black
Crackles hopping
Hissing, popping

Jolting the writers off track

River walking
Leaf is balking
Trapped by icy clear claws
Veins are etching
Thin and stretching
Beseeching an early thaw

Girl is stressing
Thoughts regressing
Perched up on snowy rocks
Mood is waning
Stop complaining
All writers get writer's block

Leaf starts moving
Veins are grooving
Taunting nature's cruel hold
Leaf gets going
Freely flowing
Writers witness it unfold

Girl succeeding
Not conceding
The doubt-filled fears and flaws
Thoughts are scrolling
Pen is rolling
Wrapped hyggely in woolen shawls

THE GIRL IN ROOM 9

Luggage hauling
Goodbyes calling
Rock, roll and meditate
Drive home raining
Sun abstaining
Room 9 contemplates her fate

FEAR OF FAILURE
by Selah Gray

Stillness
Leaves undisturbed
Stiffly bound to low-hanging limbs
Unable to dance
Without a breeze
Unable to shine
With no light

Darkness
Replaces the day
Paints the sky
Into a vacant canvas
Guiding my way

To fear
A tree split at the bottom
The risk of falling
Echoing in my mind
A nagging hiccup

Which won't stop

My thoughts
Rise like the sun
Beating down
Without escape
Haunting

My dreams
Deep in the forest of my brain
Tangled in the landscape
Embroiled in
The chronic possibility
Of failure

CONSECRATION
by Laura Lovic-Lindsay

The soot-haired boy is maybe thirteen. He
comes to these woods
humming, weaving mists through trees as he
paces the evening:
hunting a useful clearing, gathering stones into a
circle as wide

as he is tall. He chooses branches now,
according to their kind: oak,
ash, hawthorn. His hands roughen the length of
them, snapping
the leaves at their necks. He breaks them by
body lengths, tents

them in his groundcircle. In one pouch, he hides
two baby crows,
fed by his own hand for three weeks. He lights
dry tinder by the flame

of his lantern. A brief shiver, a roar and swarm
of coral-and-salmon

firestars break free in a frenzy and twist,
straining toward the tallest
branches. He positions his twin crows outside
the northern arc
with a whisper for each. They croak as he draws
Grandfather's stone

whistle from his bag, shakes the salt from it.
Three long sultry notes
and a thousand crows converge from all
directions, riding on unseen
currents, wrap themselves in the spiral of sparks.
They funnel

a whirlwind of leaves while the boy throws his
cloak to the ground,
dances the circle, coated in sweat. His own
crows' feathers surge
and thicken. The birds are pulled upward in the
rage and seat neatly

upon his shoulders, sighing. At a moment, all is
silenced—flames recede,
foreign crows depart, leaves settle. The boy
gathers whistle, lantern, cloak...
traces home his path through morning mist,
teaching his crows their names.

WHAT I DON'T KNOWABOUT NATURE
by Ramona DeFelice Long

I don't know what genus of trees grows where we went hiking. I can't recall if the flowing water we walked beside was a brook, a creek, or a stream. The fish in the water—bass or bluegill? I can never remember the difference.

In the shade, moss grows on the sides of the rocks and green stuff clings to the trees. Lichen, you called it, but it was just green gunk to me. Poisonous vines crowd the path—or maybe the vines are harmless. Flowers blossom in the brambles. They smell sweet, but their names escape me.

I watched you skim stones across the water—one, two, three hops—before sinking. The stones I tossed plopped and disappeared. I laughed, and you laughed with me.

I lie on a rock and stare up at the canopy of leaves. When you left, they were green; now they're gold, red, orange. Two fall, twirling, and settle on my stomach. I run my fingers over the moss and down to the dirt that is dry and hard. It hasn't rained since. . . I can't remember. The rock is cold against my back.

The first letter you sent from the desert had sand in the envelope. I lined up the grains on my dresser and Scotch taped them to the glass. Now the tape is fraying because I've run my fingers over and over it.

Overhead, a small brown bird hops along a limb of the golden-leafed tree. A wren? A thrush? A starling, a warbler? Long ago, you explained how to tell the seasonals from the permanent, but I watched your lips instead of listening.

The bird disappears into the canopy. I wish I'd paid attention when you talked about the birds, the fish, the plants, the trees. . . about everything.

You wrote from foreign places and told me what you could. When you came home, a flag covered your casket, hiding the glossy wood. Pine or maybe oak–what did it matter? The flag's edges were sharply creased when it was presented to me.

The bird flies off, a brown flutter under the gold. I raise my head and squint. Am I seeing what I see? Is that crazy bird making a nest, in November? The wind rustles, moves the leaves, and shows a nest of twigs, and leaves, and small shiny things not native to the woods.

WHAT I DON'T KNOW ABOUT NATURE

I pull the ribbon that's not a ribbon from my hair. It's yarn I threaded out from your old green sweater, the one you left behind for when I sleep. Every day I wear a bit of it in my hair because at night I never sleep.

I lay the yarn on the rock, like an offering. Maybe the bird will take it, and twine it in the branches, in a nest made in November, in a tree I cannot name. Or maybe it will lie on this rock, beside me, and wait to blow away.

originally published in the Fox Chase Review,
Winter 2015

TO BOLDLY GO…INTO THE WOODS
by Sherren Elias Pensiero

Cool autumn evenings in rural Ligonier
hidden from the complex energy
of all else—contemplating
the fascinating, fearful,
and ephemeral lifetimes of
to boldly go's: college, career,
marriage, children, retirement,
Widowhood.

Intrepid endeavors of reinvention
—mostly to others' expectations—
spawned yet another bold rewrite.
"This Just In. City-born and bred
wannabe writer—with an irrational
fear of wildlife, and an aversion
to being in the cold outdoors—
participates in rustic writing retreat
in the woods of the Laurel Highlands."

SHERREN ELIAS PENSIERO

A surprising, introspective week
conquering my feral fears
to the accompaniment of the
rat-a-tatting laptops rhythmically
played by my more-prolific fellow scribes.

Creating and parsing
abstract and concrete comparisons,
hiking and meditating
in a wilderness Scriptorium:
Mindfully liberating.

Metaphorical tropes of fall colors,
scented candles glazed with sweet similes
of tea and burgundy, and the
warmth of fireplace networking:
Mindfully inspiring.

Lost in my thoughts
on this last, quiet time of night,
coloring my feelings in magenta hues
of reds and blues, and
blending them into a purple haze
that no longer defines and limits me.

Rewriting restless points of view
of the dark that surrounds anticipation.
Looking deep into the eyes of local wildlife
with newfound fortitude and peace:
I have boldly gone…

Into the Woods.

THE WISP OF THE FOREST
by Larry Schardt

My fair muse, she awaits.
My loving muse, she calls.
She wisps through the forest
Without boundaries or walls.

Is she a fantasy?
Angel, fairy, or elf?
My muse bursts with magic,
Frees thoughts deep in myself.

A path through the forest
Opens gateways to dreams.
She tiptoes and flitters
Through sunrays and moonbeams.

Life's mysteries she solves
In the forest so near.
She whispers her secrets,
Silent voice I can hear.

Her beauty she dazzles,
In every leaf and tree.
Mesmerized by her spell,
Tender words set me free.

She casts knowing answers,
She makes everything clear.
Breaking down every block,
Fills my heart with her cheer.

She's just a walk away,
Every step pure pleasure.
She dances the forest
And brightens life's treasure.

I thank God for the woods,
Special place that I choose.
All prayers and blessings,
Magic home of my muse.

FOREST BATHING
by Martha Swiss

I am alone in this place that is alive, anticipating
the gift before me.
I open it slowly, with grateful breath, footsteps
and heartbeats,
then thankfully sink into the purifying molecules
of chlorophyll and humus.
I bask, now able to sense the purpose of ferns,
snakeroot, noble trees and the creek that tumbles
past my feet.

Crayfish pay me no mind in their muddy
caverns.
Trees skyrocket overhead, on a mission.
Chipmunks skitter through leaf litter
and a kingfisher pounds its teal wings heading
upstream.
I am dwarfed by the hillside vaulting from the
floodplain. Boulders and saplings cling to its
spine.

I am free to bathe here in clarified cells of
cambium, xylem and phloem.
I wring my sponge in the generosity of flora.
The stream's effervescence cleanses the tangled
energy seeping from my pores.

I celebrate my fresh spirit with a confetti of
scarlet, orange and yellow leaves that bob on the
breast of the creek
as silently,
the trees disrobe.

THE HOUR HAS COME
by Amy Walter

Like the girl who trod the loaf,
Hans Christian would be better off
telling your story.

Yet this fairy tale ended in brutality—
a girl who cannot escape her nightmare
must endure a life
of hell on earth,
a punishment in broad daylight fixating
on mistakes
less common, repetitive still,
none the less.

Be careful not to soil your shoes, little girl,
for the hour has come
for redemption,
instead misfortune lurks
in every dark corner,
despite shortcuts avoided

down this righteous path
where trust leads to temptation,
a forbidden fruit,
a crossroads,
where Eve
made the same mistake, too.

ESSAYS

SAVING THE SYCAMORES
by Teresa Futrick

It all started when Mike told the code enforcement officer he was a (expletive deleted) moron.

Well, that's not exactly right. I guess it all started when a limb from one of my sycamore trees fell on a neighbor's car. The car's owner called the borough manager's office to register a complaint, so the code enforcement officer stopped by for a quick chat. The talk ended when Mike called him a (expletive deleted) moron.

In the twenty-six years of our married life, Mike and I have talked through most major decisions—whose car to trade in, what church to attend, Maytag or Kitchen Aid appliances, what he should wear to weddings—things like that. But when it comes to "my" sycamore trees, I make the decisions.

During the early 1900s, big cities spent tens of millions of dollars to line their avenues with sycamores. By day, the sycamore's giant leaves provided a lush shade. By night, their ghostly trunks cast just enough light to keep carriages in the middle of the dark streets and off the middle of any hapless pedestrians. Few of the street trees planted in the twentieth century survive. But mine do.

On May fifth, the day after the (expletive deleted) moron conversation, we received a registered letter from the borough manager's office informing us we were in violation of Ordinance No. 1246 Property Maintenance Code, Section 183-2 Trees, which reads . . .

Every owner of property in the Borough shall be required to keep the limbs and branches of all trees growing upon such property trimmed so that no part of such limbs or branches or the foliage growing thereupon shall have a clearance of less than eight feet above the surface of the sidewalk.

Was he kidding?! The trees are ninety feet tall! The lowest limb is a good forty feet off the ground. A second registered letter arrived, this one rescinding the first and citing another part of Section 183-2.

No branches or foliage may extend from the trunk of any tree more than halfway over any street, alley or any borough right of way.

The tree in question was growing behind a stone retaining wall. If the branches extending over the street were cut off, it would topple over and my garden would be minus one sycamore. No!

My Irish went off. I could feel my hair start to frizz. My freckles exploded into blotches! I dialed my sister the lawyer as our old collie tip-toed out the screen door. He'd seen my Irish go off before. My sister said, "Calm down. Be professional. Breathe." She said, "Play the game. Just string things out until the code officer cools down." She said she'd write a letter.

The next morning another limb fell. This one hit the neighbor's daughter's car. It was a small limb that made a small dent, but she called the police. The responding officer said, "You need to do something and do it now!"

Mike found a man who would trim the tree. I cried. I bawled. I went for walks that turned into runs. I wondered what I'd wear if I had to chain myself to a tree. I wondered how people who had chained themselves to trees managed bathroom breaks.

A few days after the sycamore tree was trimmed, Mike ran into the code enforcement officer at the library. What started out as a quiet little chat-up ended in a venomous mutter. Another "(expletive deleted) moron" resulted in the registering of yet another letter from the borough manager's office. This letter again cited Section 183-2 Trees, but ended with the blunt admonition.

Your trees are still more than halfway across the street. You are hereby directed to remove this violation from your property on or before July eighth.

Trees. Plural. What exactly did "remove this violation" mean? If he wanted to push it, could the code enforcement officer make me cut down all the sycamores?

Trimming a tree in warm weather, when the sap is running, opens the tree to any disease or fungus lurking in the neighborhood. What could happen to a tree pruned twice in as many months? I was shaken to my core. That night I dreamed I was naked and shivering on our porch. The leaves that had formed a soft canopy for our house were gone. The sky was dead black. Twinkling stars had been replaced by particles of sawdust. I keened. I mourned the loss of my trees. When I woke in the morning my red eyes were not from crying, I was seeing red and I was brawling mad!

I called a friend who recommended questioning the credentials of the code enforcement officer, hiring my sister the lawyer and buying a muzzle for Mike. Another friend told me the code officer's job was to enforce the code. She said, "He can't waive a violation, that's above his pay grade. Go around him. Go over his head."

I talked to a man involved with a street tree program in a neighboring town. He told me sycamore trees don't need trimming. Stating the obvious, he said, "They're self-grooming." We hired an ISA certified arborist who sent a letter to the borough manager's office. The letter said the trees were healthy, but should not be trimmed until air temperatures were below freezing. December or January at the earliest and the latest.

I called the mayor to request a hearing in front of the borough council. I told him I'd bring my sister the lawyer. He said he'd talk to the borough manager.

While the mayor was talking to the borough manager, I talked to Mike. I told him he was relieved of duty, I was taking over as project manager and that he needed to stop being so (expletive deleted) grouchy. I scheduled a meeting with the code enforcement officer. He was professional, even cautiously nice; he said he understood why the trees were vulnerable and was willing to grant an extension until the onset of cold weather, but the trees would still have to be brought to code. All he needed was a letter requesting an extension. "How about January thirty-first?" he said.

I called the We Trim Your Trees Company in the next town over, explained the situation and asked them to come any time they weren't busy in December or January. Anytime. December came and went. The middle of January came and went. The We Trim Your Trees Company did not. No one answered the phone. I left increasingly shrill messages. Nothing. I boiled up to their office. The door was locked. A notice secured with duct tape held two messages. A cardboard sign said Out of Business. A stripe of duct tape carried the second note, "Sorry we missed you, dude. Have a nice life."

I scheduled another appointment with the code officer. He could not grant another extension. He asked if I wanted the name of a local tree trimmer, a start-up he'd used recently. I did.

That evening a young man parked in our driveway and walked around assessing my trees. A few hours later he called with a proposal. Bringing the trees to code by the end of the month would mean closing the street, a crane, a crane operator, three tree men, and $20,000. They could start January twenty-ninth and be cleaned up by the January thirty-first deadline. I made him promise not to cut an inch more than the code required.

During the early hours of January twenty-ninth, winds from the south blew in warmer air. The January thaw had never been part of the plan. What if it was too warm to cut? What if the sap started rising in the heat?

What if the work wasn't completed by the deadline? Would they really fine us $1,000 a day for each tree in violation of the code? I caved.

By 7:30 a.m., there was a light dusting of frost still glinting on the grass, the street was blocked off and the crane was in place. The stink of diesel fuel assaulted the breeze. The tree crew parked their pickups and reported for work wearing hard hats and long, heavy Carhartt coats. The *Ride of the Valkyries* was an ear-worm in my head.

Lured by the thrum of heavy machinery and the whine of chain saws, some neighbors dragged lawn chairs and coffee onto the sidewalk; tea drinkers gathered on our porch. Every now and then, a tree guy would stop for a bottle of water and shrug off his hot, heavy Carhartt. That afternoon the temperature reached a record high of seventy-eight. The men swinging from our trees worked in the full leafless sun of the January thaw, sweltering in their heavy flannel shirts.

With Mike safely locked in his office, the code enforcement officer was called to inspect the job. My trees passed muster. He gave them two thumbs-up! That evening I soothed my bruised nerves with a medicinal Schlitz or two; my hair unfrizzed and my freckles started to contract. It was over. It took a few days and a few more beers before I could stop obsessing about the trees and what could have happened to them. I realized I should have had more faith in the sycamores. They've survived road salt, micro bursts, lightning strikes and January thaws for almost a hundred years. They're wise and strong and for now, they're safe.

Until one of them decides to self-groom by bouncing another limb off a neighbor's car.

OUT OF THE WOODS
by James Robinson, Jr.

I HATE THE WOODS. Oh, I'm sorry. Was that harsh? I shouldn't have put that statement in caps. I meant to say, "I hate the woods." Does that make you feel better? Why do I hate the woods? Well, it's not the woods that I hate per se. I like trees and leaves and grass—maybe not grass; I'm allergic to grass—I just don't like all of those things in abundance. I prefer to look at them from afar, behold their majesty from a distance. Wow, am I full of shit. You get the idea.

So, at the twice-annual Mindful Writers Retreats, while my cohorts take on the great outdoors, I stay cuddled up on my inflated mattress in my dungeon-like room checking time on my iPhone. I can hear them out there laughing and joking and cajoling in the writing area filled with truckloads of snacks as I drift in and out of consciousness. I wait for them to return then I rise for breakfast. I never miss a meal although I could exist on the snacks.

You would think that the comradery, the bonding with my fellow writers would make me want to jump up, throw on my walking gear and leap into the fray. But it doesn't. Firstly, I don't have any walking gear. Secondly, I want my sleep. So, shoot me.

Then there are the physical anomalies. I have plantar fasciitis, arthritis in every joint and I suffer from the debilitating affliction known as sleep apnea. Actually, it's not all that debilitating; I've found somewhat of a remedy for it but it is a problem and, besides, I was trying to make a point. In addition to the aforementioned afflictions, I'm old. I have Medicare records to prove it. I love my writing buddies, my homies, my peeps. But I hate the woods. Nothing personal.

Part of my problem lies in the fact that I spent time in Presbyterian summer youth camps as a child. My father, a Presbyterian minister for thirty-eight years, forced me to attend these summer campsites during my formative years of seven to ten. For some reason, he took on the job of camp director at a number of these encampments.

The most vivid memories center around one in Ponca City, Oklahoma. I have to admit the food at Ponca City was good and the Olympic-size pool was magnificent. Problem was, I had this fear of water at that age. At one point, friends and fellow campsters stood around me in the magnificent pool and chanted until I put my head underwater. Is this a good way to teach a youngster how to swim? In addition, there were large tarantulas walking about on the grounds—lots of them. Everyone seemed to be amazed by their size and numbers. You'd think we would have been warned:

Those big hairy things that you see walking about are called tarantulas. Don't attempt to pick them up. They aren't poisonous but they will bite the living shit out of you. The pool opens at 10:00 am. Have fun!!

The Management

Yes, dammit, I was a Presbyterian. I hate Presbyterians. I hate the woods and I hate Presbyterians. Yeah, I said it.

There was no torture, at least of a physical nature, at these Presbyterian sites but there was mental torture, a brainwashing of sorts. In addition to the swimming, hiking, praying, and camping there was singing—always the singing, lots and lots of singing. After we ate dinner and roasted the perfunctory marshmallows, we sat around the campfire (always the campfire) and sang, gulp, Presbyterian camp songs. Yes, that's right, Presbyterians have their own camp songs. They went like this:

We are the Presbyterian kids, that's our name too,

Whenever we go out, the people always shout,

There go the Presbyterian kids, nah, nah, nah, nah, nah, nah, nah, nah

Repeat.

Do you see what I mean? While you might not consider this to be a big deal—"why is he being such a little wienie about this," you're asking—to you, I query: "How many of you can just rattle off a Catholic camp song or a Lutheran camp song?" Think about it—*We are the Muslim kids*. I don't think so. I rest my case.

So, apparently, besides the fact that I don't take solace in the great outdoors I'm also not a fan of Presbyterian music. Sometimes I feel like these songs come back to haunt me like something out of a Jason Bourne movie. Push the right buttons, say my name in a certain sequence and I'll reach for the marshmallows and start singing.

So, I come to Mindful Writers Retreats to write, meditate, eat, focus, be mindful, cajole and cohabit with friends and fellow writers. Yeah, all that good shit. But I don't come to go *Into The Woods*. Let's face it. I'm a couch potato. I don't pay for Netflix and cable for the hell of it. I hate the woods. I hate Presbyterians. I hate those damn Presbyterian songs. But I've made my peace with tarantulas. And I learned how to swim. Sometimes, you take your victories where you can get them…and in small doses.

I'm dropping a microphone.

INTO THE WOODS
by Carol Schoenig

I thoroughly enjoy the fall session of the Mindful Writers Retreat. It makes me think about all the children's stories that are set in the woods. Goldilocks went into the woods and slept in the three bears' house. Snow White ran into the woods, and Little Red Riding Hood had to go into the woods to get to Grandmother's house. These favorite children's stories all took place in the woods, not to mention the number of horror movies that took place in the woods. What is it that makes going into the woods delightful?

The retreat takes us into the woods, to enjoy the quiet, soothing language of Mother Nature. The sound of the babbling brook, songs of the birds and the swoosh of leaves as we walk through them fill me with joy. The tantalizing smells of pine, and decaying bark and earth makes me mindful of the fragile balance between life and death. The soft feel of moss on the trees reminds one of velvet. If you close your eyes and listen to the swaying leaves on trees, it sounds like you're at the ocean and the waves are going in and out. The sounds of nature bring peace to my heart, releasing my deeper, inner thoughts. In the woods, I find my lovers' deep secrets and emotions that take them down the romantic path to their love story.

Into the woods we go, to light flying wish paper and become childlike for a few days.

YOU'VE GOT MAIL!
by Linda K. Schmitmeyer

A digital notification flashes in the upper right-hand corner of my laptop. It's an email from Artists' Orchard, one of the many book agents and independent publishers to whom I've sent my manuscript. I've written a memoir about coping with my husband's mental illness when our children were young; now I'm looking for a publisher.

I started writing *Rambler: A family pushes through the fog of mental illness* when people spoke in whispers about such things. "I won't share details of what happened to Steve," a friend wrote in a note she sent me shortly after his breakdown. My friend, a nurse, meant well, but her message reinforced my own misunderstanding about mental illness. That it was something to be ashamed of, a weakness in one's character. I don't fault my friend; there was no Internet to search or TV ads about it when Steve got sick. And I struggled for years to understand how changes in his thinking and behavior were symptoms of an illness.

Life had been ticking along nicely for our family. We were well into the second decade of marriage and quite happy. Steve worked as a mechanical engineer, and I was mostly a stay-at-home mom. I taught writing part-time at the local community college to keep connected to my teaching life, which I'd put on hold when the kids were born. Then everything changed; I became the family breadwinner, a single mother of sorts, and the caregiver for a man whose moods rose and fell like the wind.

In *Rambler,* I write about wrapping my mind around these changes:

If disease and disorders were coded by color, then gray would best represent mental illness. Achromatic, the color of smoke; where black and white overlap, where health and sickness intersect. Steve's manic depression, as bipolar disorder was called in the mid-1990s, didn't manifest in any medically discernable manner, like a lump on a breast or an elevated PSA number. Instead, it entered our family life slowly over a period of several years, an indefinable force that disrupted routines and changed our lives without my knowing it was happening. I never thought of Steve's quickening temper as a symptom of an illness; I blamed it on the stress of several job changes during a short period of time and the pressure to provide for our growing family.

During the next several years, as doctors searched for a combination of medications to quiet Steve's mind, we still had periods of normalcy, where the kids played soccer and we attended parent-teacher conferences. But there was also chaos and confusion. Like Steve abandoning his family responsibilities to focus solely on getting his former boss removed from office. Or me excusing Steve's angry outbursts as the symptom of an illness while punishing my thirteen-year-old for failing to control his emotions. The most difficult times were when Steve was psychotic and left in his old Rambler to drive aimlessly for hundreds of miles without telling anyone where he was.

With the right medications, Steve's mood eventually stabilized and his thinking cleared. Shortly after that, I wrote an account of our family's experience, a 14,000-word document that became the basis for my memoir. Over the next nineteen years, through innumerable starts and stops and a great deal of handwringing, I wrote *Rambler*. The process of writing such an intimate family story pushed me well beyond the early days of Steve's illness, when I spoke in whispers about it.

Now that the book is finished, I've sent it to agents and publishers. Some have responded, thanking me for the opportunity to review my manuscript, BUT...

Will Artists' Orchard's response be the same? I pause before clicking on the email, savoring possibility.

Dealing with the multitude of changes and roller-coaster of emotions associated with Steve's illness—from confusion and uncertainty to determination and acceptance—I've come to see life as a series of connecting paths. Some are in sunshine; others take us through dark woods. During the worst days of Steve's illness, when I was deep in despair and the path wasn't clear, I willed myself forward, lifting one leg and then the other as I moved through the shadows. But with the passing of time and a determination rooted in my love for Steve and our family, the darkness lifted and I moved toward the light. Living with a loved one's mental illness helped me understand that we don't always get to choose the path we walk; I also learned how to be okay with the one I'm on.

I click on Artists' Orchard's email, and the path pivots again.

*Linda K. Schmitmeyer's memoir, *Rambler: A family pushes through the fog of mental illness*, will be published by The Artists' Orchard in Fall 2018.*

INTO THE WOODS: LESSONS LEARNED AND LOVED
by Denise Weaver

No matter the season, spirituality reigns as I enter the woods, through thoughts and ideas, emotions and sensations, revelations and experiences. Sometimes it unfurls gradually like the tightly curled fronds of the fiddlehead fern as I meander without purpose. Or, as I hike with intention, it can overtake me as quickly as heavy rains on snow produce a new, fast-running stream. Each trek, I know I can find what I'm looking for, including the unexpected.

Winter: It seems as though all plants and animal life are dormant, flora is not growing, I don't see many animals scampering through the woods, don't hear many birds chattering and calling and singing. Bears, I hope, are sound asleep deep in hibernation. Yet I hear the jackhammering of a pileated woodpecker, pounding away at the dying oak tree, the sound reverberating through the otherwise silent forest. The tracks of a deer's hooves having dug down into the snow to access the acorns lying below are blatantly visible. A spider—who knows how it has survived the cold temperatures—skitters across the hard crust of snow following a sunny day. Delicate yet sturdy leaves and stems pop up through the snow, looking like plants germinating from seeds planted in the warm soil of late spring. The air smells exceptionally clean, almost devoid of aroma, so fresh and unmarred. This feels like a new beginning, a clean slate, not the dead season.

Spring: This is the time of year when I expect to see new life, new growth, and experience an awakening of sensual and tactile experiential elements. Flowers are beginning to bloom, daffodils (my favorite) foretelling the promise of abundant sunshine. There's new life in faith relaunching within hearts with spring holy days. Lawns develop a verdant sheen as grass comes back to life and begins to grow again. Leaves bud on trees and shrubs, birds are returning from their southward expedition, small woodland creatures reappear, dashing to and fro—rabbits and squirrels and chipmunks and skunks and porcupine. The scents of flowers blooming, cleansing rains, and the earth warming, all mix and mingle, tantalizing the nostrils. Squirrels chattering, birds calling, and off in the distance an owl hooting in the early morn' create a dance of sound. Everyone is busy preparing for the growing and mating season. The drool-producing scent of honeysuckle, so brief but enticing, joins the sounds of the spring peepers, rushing us onward to new beginnings. And yet, there is the slow dying of winter's solitude, the peace of just being.

Summer: Ah, summer arrives bringing a mix of activity and relaxation. It's vacation time, with play, travel, adventure, sunshine, and siestas in the sultry heat. Smells of last night's barbeque linger at the edge of the woods. Sunlight filtering through the leaves of the tall oaks rising high into the sky form a canopy for the city of wildlife underneath. Early morning brings much activity, while during afternoon even the busiest of bees seems to rest in the sweltering but still welcome heat of the day. The scents of mountain laurel of early summer and, later, sweet roses fill the air. In the heat, a bit of respite coolness can be found under the leaves, near the stream, while hearing the water gently lap away at the edges of the bank inducing a lazy and lingering comfort. It's a quieter time in the summer afternoon, low hums of insects, a soft swish of a fern, and only occasional bird twitter as all creatures seem to slow for a break. Most flora have reached their peak of growth and are now beginning to laze about, their work nearly complete. Summer is an incongruent but compatible weaving of activity and rest.

Autumn: If forced to choose, I likely would name this season as my favorite. It evokes nesting and nestling, stockpiling and storing, transforming and transitioning, coloring and conforming, chilling and changing, falling and forming, and most importantly, giving thanks and assessing. Squirrels storing nuts, bears filling up, acorns falling, sweet decaying aroma of dying and drying leaves, and the occasional smoky scent of a neighbor burning the deciduous detritus all signal an end. However, flocks of birds in formation with a leader calling orders, embark on a new adventure. Cooler temperatures alternating with warm sunshine giving us early fall heat and late autumn cold rains command new winter coats for many animals. Sounds of hunters nearby, shots fired in hope of acquiring provisions in the form of venison and turkey outperform the wails of a train whistle in the distance. Dry leaves crunch underfoot or scurry unscathed from the wind. It is a time for dying and for renewing, ending and starting anew.

In each of the seasons, patterns form and appear: animal tracks in snow or mud, water flow after a rain, variegation in vegetation, striations in rock, bird migration paths, animal navigation trails, cadence of cricket chirps and frog croaks, moss formations, colorations in butterfly and bird wings, and shadows of sunlight filtering through leaves.

Throughout all the patterns, sights, sounds, aromas, tastes, and feelings, everywhere I see glimpses of the Divine. Going into the woods affords me contemplation, revelation, solace, peace, inspiration, comfort, and joy, all the handiwork of God.

From each encounter, I learn lessons on some topic or quality of being that serves me well. The last leaf clinging tenaciously to a limb, hanging there through winter's winds, teaches me to not give up. Observing the determination of daffodils to punch upward through the soil and snow, I witness and absorb strength. In varied and unique ways, I learn the importance and need for these additional qualities: power, rest, community, individualism, solitude, gathering, preparation, attention, mindfulness, and above all, celebration, appreciation, and love.

THE DIRTIEST, MOST DIVINE SANCTUARY
by Michele Savaunah Zirkle

The sanctuary in which I've experienced the most divine bliss is landscaped with mud, ticks and decaying leaves. Pollen drifts across the rocky path that's all but impassable due to a fallen birch tree. Birds tweet the hymns in this wilderness chapel—a woodpecker is rhythm-keeper and a crow provides the baritone.

Each tree strives majestically toward the heavens like a steeple, each branch bowing in supplication to the Source of all light. Sunlight flickers like a candle through the trees, casting shadows onto the trail and the underbrush.

A chipmunk takes its place on a boulder while I curl up on a log. I sit reverently awaiting the message I'm bound to hear in such a profundity of silence.

The only rumors here are whispered by the wind, the only offering plate passed is a nut from one squirrel to another. Living fully present in each moment is my oblation even when my wallet is empty. I hope I respect all life and all people as much as this enchanted cathedral seems to honor me.

I imagine every form of creature—every insect and plant, every oak and evergreen—feels as welcome here as I do. This immaculate, messy canopy of raw life doesn't mind my unshaven legs and muddy tennis shoes.

Judgment rests on my shoulders alone. Here I ask myself if I'm living my highest truth—if I'm inhaling grace and exhaling gratitude. Questions stir deep within; pangs of remorse for past shortcomings surf alongside joy for the abundance of love.

I listen to the stream gurgle and remember my baptism. As I was being dunked into that cold river when I was seven, I wondered how water could wash away anything other than the dirt on my feet from running barefoot along the riverbank.

Now, I feel that it can't. Water can't wash away my past any more than a cascading waterfall can shape my future. Mud could wash away my faults just as effectively, just like it made the blind man see. Intention and faith are what matter.

I slide off my rustic pew and sink my hands into the ground beneath me, feeling the grass and the dirt between my fingers, thankful that before the first stone church was built, there was this—the exquisite sanctuary designed by an ultimately forgiving Mother Nature.

MUSIC

WALK IN THE WOODS
by Gail Oare

Walk in the Woods

for Scottish Smallpipes

Gail Oare

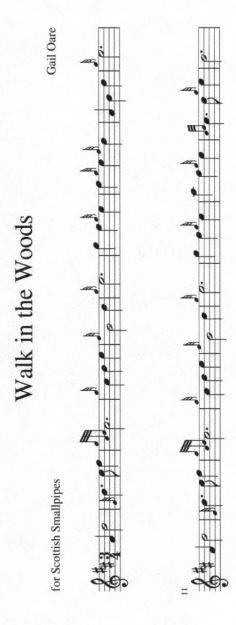

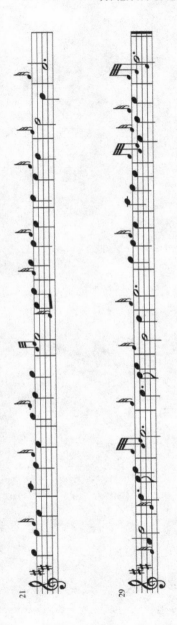

WALKING MEDITATION

Walking Meditation
by Lori M. Jones

"Keep close to nature's heart...and break clear away, once in a while, and climb a mountain or spend a week in the woods. Wash your spirit clean." ~ John Muir

Like seated meditation, walking meditation is a productive way to ignite your senses and spark your creativity. Take a quiet stroll around your block or in the woods to rid yourself of artistic blocks or generate the creative flow. Countless scientific studies have been conducted on the creative benefits of walking and engaging with nature.

Start off with light stretching and deep breathing. After a few long breaths, close your eyes and visualize your work in progress. Once you've focused on your piece, narrow in on the scene you wish to develop. Then, see the character at the center of the scene. Ask that character what are his goals, what is she trying to accomplish, what obstacles are standing in his way?

In seated meditation, when unwelcome or foreign thoughts take over your mind, it's suggested that the meditator acknowledge them and let them go. When mindfully walking, it might be a good idea to come up with your own mantra to repeat when your thoughts become scattered and your mind jumps off track. One good mantra is, "I give to the universe and the universe gives to me." Design your own mantra to use when the flow takes you off course.

One technique that helps to re-focus your thoughts is to zero in on your footsteps and sync your breathing with your footfalls. Once you're in tune with body and your breath, re-focus on your work in progress. Sometimes repeating the mantra *Body, Breath, Book...Body, Breath, Book* will help clear your artistic canvas.

Then let the characters speak to each other and to you. Interact with them, ask them questions, provoke them and let the scene unfold. Tune into nature's surroundings and breathe in the fresh air as your blocks crumble away and fresh ideas swirl around right along with your pumping blood.

It's a good idea to take along a small notepad and pen to jot down ideas. After a mile of walking, find a place to sit and write down your new thoughts.

"If you are seeking creative ideas, go out walking. Angels whisper to a man when he goes for a walk." ~ Raymond Inmon

CONTRIBUTORS

LORRAINE BONZELET, a retired engineer, has always been a picture book enthusiast at heart. She spends her free time analyzing picture books and writing stories. Her passion for writing is tied with her passion for travel; both of which she does whenever and wherever she can. She also enjoys running, kayaking, reading, and taking pictures of odd, interesting and unusual things. She resides in Maryland with her loving husband, two incredible teenage daughters, a howling miniature beagle, two tabby cats and wildlife running amok in the yard.

WENDE DIKEC is the author of three young adult novels and seven adult books written under her pen name, Abigail Drake. She adores snow, and secretly thinks getting trapped in a cozy cabin in the woods for a few months might not be so bad. After living abroad for many years, in places with very little snow, she finally settled in Beaver, Pennsylvania, with her husband, three sons, and a Labrador retriever named Capone. Capone does not share her love of things cold and wintery, and would prefer to live on a beach and drink rum punch.

KIM FORD is a business entrepreneur and writer from Pittsburgh. Her latest published work was in *The Missing Piece* magazine, an interactive, digital magazine published out of East Yorkshire, England. Through the Foundation of Hope non-profit, she mentors female inmates at the Allegheny County Penitentiary located in Pittsburgh, PA and does volunteer work with victims of sex trafficking at Living in Liberty. She is a member of Sisters in Crime and Pennwriters. Kim writes under the pen name of Selah Gray.

TERESA FUTRICK, who grew up across the street from a swimming pool but still doesn't know how to swim, is cautiously dipping her toe in the water with *Saving The Sycamores*, an almost true story. She has seen her share of trees alive and content with their place in the world, only to be felled because of spite, neglect or codes. She writes a bi-weekly garden column for *The Altoona Mirror*, and lives in dread of the reader who will drop by to see her garden which is usually in a complete state of dishabille, as is she.

KIMBERLY KURTH GRAY was born and raised in Baltimore where she finds daily inspiration for her writing. The winner of the William F. Deeck-Malice Domestic 2009 Grant for Unpublished Writers and a 2017 Hruska Fellowship, she is a member of Sisters in Crime,

Guppies and Pennwriters. Her short stories have been published in Cat and Mouse Press and Level Best Anthologies. In addition to working on a historical novel and writing short stories, she appears monthly as The Detective's Daughter on the Wicked Cozy Authors blog.

EILEEN ENWRIGHT HODGETTS is working on the fifth book of her four-book Arthurian saga, *Excalibur Rising*. She is also the scriptwriter on a soon to be released movie and author of a number of stage plays. She is a happy transplant from the United Kingdom to the United States by way of Africa and her travels are often reflected in her characters and the places where they can be found. She has attended every Mindful Writers Retreat so far and the company of other writers has changed her life and her writing forever. www.eileenenwrighthodgetts.com.

HILARY HAUCK is a writer, translator and poet living in Pennsylvania. She has lived in three countries, hiked in the Himalayas, ridden a dromedary at sunrise in the Sahara, and watched bodies being burned on the banks of the River Ganges. Her travels greatly influence her writing, and she never tires of exploring the cultural and sensorial lenses through which people experience the world. A recent graduate of RULE XVI, Hilary is current president of Pennwriters, and co-founder of the Allegheny Regional Festival of Books. She gains immense inspiration from the Mindful Writers Retreats, and writes about mindfully finding #storyeverywhere at www.hilaryhauck.com.

LARRY IVKOVICH's speculative fiction has been published in over twenty online and print publications. His published novels include books one through three in his urban fantasy series, The Spirit Winds Quartet (*The Sixth Precept*, *Warriors of the Light*, and *Orcus Unchained*) from IFWG Publishing. Self-published science fiction novel, *Magus Star Rising*, is now available from Amazon. A finalist in the L. Ron Hubbard's Writers of the Future Contest, Larry was also the 2010 recipient of the CZP/Rannu Fund Award for Fiction. Larry lives in Coraopolis, PA with his incredible wife Martha and wonder cats Trixie and Milo. He is a member of Parsec, WorD, Mindful Writers East and North, Pennwriters, and the Taoist Tai Chi Society of the U.S.A. Visit his website at www.larryivkovich.com.

LORI M. JONES is freelance writer and an award-winning author of women's & children's fiction. Her first children's book, *Riley's Heart Machine*, was released in 2012 and was inspired by her own daughter's heart defect. *Confetti the Croc* followed in 2014 along with her debut novel, *Renaissance of the Heart,* which was awarded the silver medal by READERS' FAVORITES in women's fiction. Her second novel, *Late for Fate,* was released in 2016 and her first middle grade novel, *Freaky Heart*, is currently on submission. Lori is represented by literary agent Gina Panettieri of Talcott Notch. Lori sits on the national board of directors for The Children's Heart Foundation and is the president of Pennsylvania Chapter.

She enjoys traveling to schools to deliver assemblies on writing stories from the heart. She resides in her hometown of Pittsburgh with her husband, two daughters, dog and bunny. Visit her website at www.lorimjones.com.

LAURA LOVIC LINDSAY left Penn State in 1993 with an English degree in hand but no idea how to apply it. A dare from her brother led her to the world of short stories and poetry. Living in tiny towns along the Allegheny River, she gleans ideas from the waters and forest that always seem to surround her. Her children and dogs keep her grounded...or attempt to.

Contributor and anthology editor RAMONA DEFELICE LONG writes short fiction, creative nonfiction, personal essays, prose poetry, and is crossing over to novel writing. Her work has appeared in literary, regional, and juvenile publications, and she has received artist fellowships and grants from the Pennsylvania State Arts Council, the Delaware Division of the Arts, the Virginia Center for Creative Arts, the Mid-Atlantic Arts Foundation, and the SCBWI. Her short story "Voices" was nominated for a Pushcart Prize in 2017, and in 2015, her artist journey was selected by the National Endowment for the Arts to represent Delaware on the United States of Arts map. Ramona is a transplanted Southerner now living in Delaware. She maintains a literary website at www.ramonadef.com.

MARYALICE MELI lives in Steelers/Pirates/Penguins country, aka Pittsburgh, PA, and has written nonfiction in past careers in education and journalism. She earned a master's degree in writing popular fiction at Seton Hill University. Now retired, she writes short and flash fiction, children's stories, middle-grade mysteries, and has begun reading all the books on her shelves designated *TBR when there's time*. She placed third in Pennwriters's 2014 short fiction contest and had two short stories published in Rehoboth Writers Guild anthologies. She's also been published online in Every Day Fiction, InfectiveINk and Untied Shoelaces of the Mind.

GAIL OARE is retired from a career in science and educational publishing. After several years of producing training films, technical manuals, marketing materials and magazines, she was given the opportunity to establish a multimillion-dollar science publishing business for an international organization and ran the operation for twenty-five years. A life-long creative writer, she now concentrates on writing and publishing short stories and poetry and occasional science magazine feature articles. She also began exploring haiku, senryu, haiga and haibun several years ago. Over a hundred of these pieces appear in journals and anthologies. She was recently accepted as a poet in both the Living Haiku Anthology and the Haiku Registry. In her spare time, she is learning to play the Scottish smallpipes and has returned to her musical roots of guitar and English concertina. She and her husband,

Mike, a retired engineering marketing manager, have two grown children who work in publishing and the arts.

KIM PIERSON lives in Western Pennsylvania with her husband and four sons, but grew up in Wisconsin, not far from the woods that inspired her short story. Trained as both a lawyer and a librarian, she drinks vats of decaf coffee, reads too late into the night, and provides a loving but messy home to a Havanese pup with trust issues.

If life imitates art, then SHERREN (SHERRIE) PENSIERO'S life mirrors the fictional Jessica Fletcher of "Murder, She Wrote" fame: English teacher, writer, busybody, amateur sleuth, busybody, college professor, busybody, widow, and bestselling author. Well, except for the bestselling author part. After thirty-one years as a high school Language Arts teacher, Sherrie took an early retirement to begin a second career as a writer. She founded The Write Solution, a home-based consulting firm that produced well-honed writing and editing solutions for companies and individuals. In addition to operating the business, she served as an adjunct writing professor at Allegany College of MD, and a work-for-hire writer/editor for several community agencies. Sherrie is the co-author of *Self-Esteem for Old Broad*s and the sole author of "The BROAD View" newspaper column. She is spending her second retirement developing her own writing style for the creative nonfiction genre.

CARA REINARD is an author of women's fiction and domestic suspense. *Pretty Dolls and Hand Grenades* and *Last Doll Standing* were published in 2016 through The Wild Rose Press. Cara is employed in the pharmaceutical industry and currently lives with her husband and two children in the Pittsburgh area.

JAMES ROBINSON, JR. hails from Pittsburgh, PA. He has written both fiction and non-fiction. His first book, *Fighting the Effects of Gravity: A Bittersweet Journey Into Middle Life*, is a humorous look at midlife filled with autobiographical anecdotes. *Gravity* won an Indie Book Award. His fiction consists of a three-book series chronicling the life of The Johnson Family. Mr. Robinson's book, *Death of a Shrinking Violet* consists of thirteen humorous essays.

LARRY SCHARDT loves sharing joy, kindness, and compassion. His passion is people. Larry encourages everyone to live with gratitude, thrive with gusto, and explore the world with a sense of wonder. He is an author, speaker, and the creator of the *Success That Rocks* series. Dr. Schardt invites you to connect via his daily blog at Facebook/larry.schardt. He is also a professor at Penn State. He loves socializing, walking, reading, music, and the outdoors. Visit his website at www.LarrySchardt.com. Peace, Love, and Rock 'n' Roll!!!

LINDA K. SCHMITMEYER is an author and educator. Her first full-length manuscript, *Rambler*, is being released by Artists' Orchard in Fall 2018. The memoir traces her experience as the mother of three young children caring for a husband with a severe mental illness. An award-winning features editor and former newspaper columnist, Linda has received honors for essays based on *Rambler*, including a writing fellowship from the Staunton Farm Foundation. Her essay, "My Mantra," was published in Creative Nonfiction Foundation's *Writing Away the Stigma*; it also was a guest blog post on the National Children's Mental Health Network's website. Linda is a freelance writer for university alumni magazines; she's currently writing a series for Carnegie Mellon's School of Computer Science on how artificial intelligence is being used to tackle global problems. She teaches writing part-time at Point Park University in Pittsburgh. She and her husband, Steve, live in western Pennsylvania.

CAROL SCHOENIG used to joke with co-workers that when she retired she was going to sit on a beach and write scintillating romance novels. Married for fifty years, Carol spends time with her husband and two grown sons and five grandchildren. She reads, sews and sings in the choir. She believes you're never too old to pursue your dreams. After she retired she wrote her debut novel, which was released in March 2017 and won the New York Big Book Award. She writes romance novels.

Bestselling author, KATHLEEN SHOOP, holds a PhD in reading education and has more than twenty years of experience in the classroom. She writes historical fiction, women's fiction and romance. Shoop's novels have garnered various awards in the Independent Publisher Book Awards (IPPY), Eric Hoffer Book Awards, Indie Excellence Awards, Next Generation Indie Book Awards, Readers' Favorite and the San Francisco Book Festival. Kathleen has been featured in *USA Today* and the *Writer's Guide to 2013*. Her work has appeared in *The Tribune-Review*, four *Chicken Soup for the Soul* books and *Pittsburgh Parent* magazine. Kathleen coordinates Mindful Writing Retreats and is a regular presenter at conferences for writers. She lives in Oakmont, Pennsylvania, with her husband and two children. For more information, visit her website at www.kshoop.com and connect with her on Facebook as Kathleen Shoop.

After a thirty-year career in technical writing, editing, and publishing, MARTHA SWISS now pursues her love of garden writing and design. She is a columnist with *Pennsylvania Gardener* magazine and her articles have appeared in *The American Gardener, Fine Gardening, Grow* (the magazine of the Pennsylvania Horticultural Society), the *Pittsburgh Post-Gazette*, and publications of the *Pittsburgh Botanic Garden*. She enjoys writing haiku and poetry, and is writing a mystery with—what else—a gardener as a main character. Like her character Takumi Nakano, Martha became hopelessly lost in the woods at her first Mindful Writers Retreat. She blogs at plantsomejoy.com.

AMY WALTER is a former journalist turned reading specialist who spends her days surrounded by books, and her nights surrounded by Yorkshire terriers. Born and raised in the Steel City of Pittsburgh, Pennsylvania, Amy ventured north to settle in the rural outskirts in the small, albeit bubbly town, of Grove City, Pennsylvania. A published essayist, fiction enthusiast, and accomplished teacher, Amy's first published poem is "The Hour Has Come." She is concurrently working on publishing a chapbook of poetry and a young adult novel.

The founder of Mindful Writers Groups, MADHU BAZAZ WANGU depicts her reverence and admiration of natural beauty in her award-winning paintings, novels and short stories. Writing stories for this anthology is continuation of her awe for the power of nature. Her debut novel, *The Immigrant Wife*, was an Indie Excellence Award Winner and Next Generation Indie Book Award finalist. She leads Mindful Writers Group sessions in person in Western Pennsylvania and the Online Mindful Writers Group via Facebook. For twenty-five years Dr. Wangu taught Buddhist and Hindu Art at Wellesley College, University of Rhode Island and University of Pittsburgh. Her books on Buddhist and Hindu art have appeared in India and United States, as has her fiction. Once every year she travels with her husband, Manoj Wangu, around the world. They enjoy the adventure of exploring remote places such as Lhasa in Tibet, Alexandria in Egypt and Matobo in Zimbabwe. Visit her website at www.madhubazazwangu.com.

DENISE WEAVER is a freelance writer, a *summa cum laude* graduate of the University of Pittsburgh, and a former library director. With nearly 200 published articles in local and regional magazines, she particularly enjoys interviewing others for personality profiles. She also serves as a copy editor and reader for *Hippocampus Magazine*. A co-founder of Allegheny Regional Festival of Books and a Pennwriters board member, Denise's joy of writing developed from a fifth-grade history class assignment. She had so much fun with the project that she's been playing with words ever since. Having placed as a finalist/honorable mention in several memoir contests, she eagerly awaits her first, first-prize award. Denise enjoys photography, cooking, and traveling, and once performed on stage at Carnegie Hall. She lives in the beautiful Laurel Highlands of Pennsylvania with her husband and their golden retriever, Murphy O'Malley.

After teaching high school English for twenty years, MICHELE SAVAUNAH ZIRKLE wrote and released her first novel, *Rain No Evil*, which won WV Writer's Inc. Honorable Mention as a short story. "The River Runs Through my Blood," took first place in Mountain Ink Literary Journal short fiction contest, and she has published several vignettes in *The Journal of Health and Human Experience*, including "Healing Hands," which describes how energy healing helped her to break a self-defeating cycle and transform her life. In addition to hosting a weekly radio show, *Life Speaks*, on AIR radio,

Michele writes inspirational columns for several Ohio Valley Publishing newspapers. She is a graduate of Concord College and Marshall Graduate School and is currently pursuing her doctorate in metaphysics.